REMOVING MANAGERIAL BARRIERS TO EFFECTIVE POLICE LEADERSHIP

A Study of Executive Leadership and Executive Management in Big-City Police Departments

By
Norman H. Stamper, Ph.D.

This report is published by PERF as a service to its members
and the general public. The opinions and recommendations
expressed in this paper are those of the author and do not
necessarily represent those of the PERF membership.

Cover Design by Fitzgerald & Swaim
Copyright © 1992, Police Executive Research Forum
Library of Congress Catalog Number: 92-61460
ISBN Number: 1-878734-29-6

Second Printing 1996

DEDICATION

To the men and women who police America's big cities. You have a right to the best leadership your bosses can provide.

FOREWORD

Norm Stamper's **Removing Managerial Barriers to Effective Police Leadership** challenges law enforcement chief executives to do some soul-searching. It forces us to determine if we are, in fact, who we profess to be when it comes to running our agencies. **Removing Managerial Barriers** causes the reader to think about how police executives are viewed by others, and provides a model that acts as a lens, focusing the reader on different ways to view leadership and management—from both personal and organizational perspectives.

In developing this model, Stamper carefully guides the reader through an analysis of the professed values and behaviors of major city police chief executives. He analyzes the ability of major city chiefs to discriminate effectively between their role as a leader and their role as a manager through a survey in which respondents quantified and prioritized leadership and management practices. The same survey questions were posed to the chiefs' immediate assistants, allowing Stamper to explore the complex relationship between a chief administrator's stated values and the chief's actual daily practices, as viewed by the individuals closest to the chief.

Stamper also provides a clear and concise analysis of law enforcement managerial and leadership development, describing the "waves of reform" that have taken place in policing over the years. His research is thorough and will expand the reader's insight into the sometimes slow and arduous emergence of contemporary law enforcement management practices and leadership philosophies.

As each new philosophy of leadership and management has been introduced to the field, innovative and progressive chiefs have embraced the new concepts and stepped forward to lead and manage ever more complex police operations. Others, fearing they would place themselves in harm's way, have maintained the status quo and become caretakers (or worse) until the danger has subsided. Despite the reluctance of some executives to move forward, progress has been steady, and solid principles have been developed by integrating new thinking with the old.

Stamper again challenges old ways of thinking and offers new alternatives. He professes that strong executive leadership has been "structured out" of police administration, and proceeds analytically, statistically, and logically to persuade us to consider a new organizational model of leadership and management. His model calls for a more appropriate separation of roles and tasks between the chief executive as leader and the chief's assistants as managers. Stamper provides a model for the future for those who have the belief, confidence, commitment, and courage to pursue true police leadership.

In the end, one question remains: Can contemporary chief law enforcement executives separate leadership and management functions after years of viewing both aspects of organizational life as synonymous and virtually interchangeable? The thought that police executives must focus much more on being leaders than managers can shake the very foundation of long-held values that, for years, have compelled us to be immersed in the daily management and operations of our departments. Can we let go?

Stamper encourages us all to consider his model of executive leadership and executive management, and to accept the need to make a "fundamental paradigm shift." Stamper cautions that our jobs will not get any easier. He stresses the need for all chief executives to work on making our successors better educated, trained, and prepared to lead our nation's law enforcement agencies. He makes an excellent case for trying his model of leadership and management—a model for success.

James J. Carvino
Chief of Police
Boise, Idaho
September 1992

ACKNOWLEDGMENTS

This research, originally conducted as part of a doctoral dissertation, was motivated by a desire to contribute something of importance to the cause of reasoned and responsible police work. If that happens, it will have been because of support I have received from many people.

From the days of design, data gathering, testing and retesting, writing, and rewriting, I would like to thank Dr. Robert H. Lauer, Dr. Morris S. Spier, Dr. Jeanette C. Lauer, Dr. Dale Hamreus, Bud Emerson, Suzanne Foucault, Dr. Joyce Ross, Dr. Trudy Sopp, Dr. Rick Ross, Cynthia Hilliard, and Norm Borgen. A special thanks to Dr. Ruben Rumbaut, friend and mentor, who helped me comprehend the meaning of my own study.

Former chief Bill Kolender and current chief of police of the San Diego Police Department Bob Burgreen were instrumental to the development of this research. Each gave me the trust, the latitude, and the support necessary to probe police executive leadership on a national scale, and to complete the sensitive body of work.

Thanks are also owed to those hundreds of police officers throughout the country, especially in my own home town, who have found the courage to question their bosses, to speak clearly and honestly of their observations about executive behavior. I am particularly indebted to those who have questioned my own positions and practices. Like most, I suspect, I learn more from a single mistake than a dozen successes.

Thanks, too, to the Police Executive Research Forum (PERF), and for the help and encouragement I received from Darrel Stephens, Bill Geller, and Martha Plotkin. PERF arranged to have Bill Falcon edit the original dissertation and turn it into this publication. I appreciate Mr. Falcon's skillful

editing—and his patience. Finally, I thank my wife, Dr. M.
Lisa Berglund, a remarkably insightful psychologist whose
own work in organizations has served as a model of caring and
effective change.

RESEARCH SUMMARY

To determine the values and behavior of America's big-city police chief executives, 52 big-city* chiefs and 92 of their immediate assistants from 28 states responded to a 100-item questionnaire pertaining to leadership and management practices or beliefs. Each questionnaire item was in the form of a statement, with which respondents indicated their strong agreement, strong disagreement, or something in-between. The chief executive officers were asked whether they *should do* what the 100 questionnaire items suggested. The chiefs' immediate assistants were asked whether they perceived that their bosses *actually do* what the questionnaire items described.

Respondents' data were analyzed in order to address four major research questions, listed below with the survey-based answers.

1. What do America's big-city police chiefs profess to value in relation to their community and organizational responsibilities?

The chiefs placed an extremely high value on the importance of sharing a vision of the future, encouraging and practicing openness and honesty, developing and challenging employees, creating an atmosphere of teamwork and open communication, helping employees get the job done, and recognizing excellence in performance. They also profess a commitment to encouraging questioning and criticism of agency policies, working closely with the communities they serve (which includes a willingness to invite citizen input on policy matters), adopting an intuitive and creative approach to their work, and taking a firm stand against discriminatory practices.

*Surveyed chiefs serve populations of at least 200,000.

vii

2. Is there a distinction in the relative importance the chiefs attach to executive leadership versus executive management functions or tasks?

The chiefs perceive a significant difference between their executive leadership functions and their management functions, believing that the leadership functions are much more deserving of their personal time and attention than are the management tasks. However, the scores for both the leadership and the management items of the survey were quite high (well above the neutral midpoint), suggesting (1) that the chiefs may not make much of a distinction in actual practice between the two functions and, therefore, (2) that both deserve the *personal* attention of the chief executive.

3. Is the executive behavior of the police chiefs, as viewed by their immediate assistants, consistent with their professed values?

According to their immediate assistants, the behavior of chiefs is not consistent with the values they expressed on the survey. This is particularly true of the leadership items. The gap between the chiefs' opinions and the assistants' observations was considerably narrower on the management items, but there is still evidence of a tendency for the chiefs to be much more involved in the technical and procedural aspects of the managerial process than they themselves believe is appropriate.

4. Are there differences in the professed values or the observed behavior of the police chiefs based on individual or contextual demographic variables?

While statistical significance was not well established in the relationship between individual and contextual demographics and responses to the survey, several trends emerged. For example, chiefs who are more likely to report an inclination toward the leadership functions are significantly more highly educated. They are also younger. They have been in police work for less time, have less tenure as chiefs, head the smallest of the large agencies (in population only, not in square miles), and run agencies with fewer sworn personnel.

To the detriment of leadership functions, police chief executives are inclined to become personally involved in many management tasks and to exhibit cautious and reactive behavior directed toward avoiding mistakes and maintaining the status quo. That orientation, in contrast to a more creative approach to organizational leadership, works against not only their success as leaders but also their professional survival.

As practiced today in many law enforcement agencies, executive leadership and executive management are virtually indistinguishable. The chief and the immediate assistant handle the same paperwork and participate, in roughly equal amounts of time, in common decision-making and problem-solving activities; with the exception of most ceremonial and political activities (the principal domain of the chief executive), their roles are, by and large, interchangeable.

In contrast, executive leadership and executive management are presented here as two separate and clearly distinguishable dimensions of big-city police administration; indeed, they represent two different jobs altogether.

A key dimension characterizing police executive leadership is that the leader is an activist, a doer, and one who inspires a shared vision of the future and establishes expectations for the kind of behavior that is expected from all employees. The leader's behavior communicates integrity and credibility. The police chief executive, as a leader, lets agency personnel know that they are important and never forgets that the purpose of the agency is to protect and to serve the community. Accordingly, chiefs must spend a large percentage of their time in their respective communities in order to better assess needs.

As a leader, the chief is one who not only tolerates but also appreciates questioning and criticism of agency policies and practices.

The executive management function is the responsibility of the assistant chief—in the sense of managing the agency's day-to-day operations. But the assistant chief does not operate autonomously; everything he or she does, or does not do, must be seen by the organization as aligned with the thinking, the vision, and the philosophy of the chief of police.

While a clear distinction is drawn between executive leadership and executive management, the two functions must overlap in certain respects. For example, budgeting might be seen as the responsibility of the assistant chief, but the chief executive would probably want to establish parameters and set up a mechanism for regular briefings on budget status.

Just as it makes sense to separate the leadership functions from the management functions at the executive level so also would it be wise to do that at other levels of the organization and for precisely the same reason—to strengthen both management and leadership.

Executive leadership has been "structured" out of police administration. The time has come for a more powerful form of big-city police leadership, one that can make American policing the kind of respected and respectful institution it struggles to be.

At a time when police executive leadership has never been more demanding—or more important—comes evidence that many of America's police chiefs are simply not practicing what they preach. This conclusion, supported by extensive research into the "professed values versus the observed behavior" of 52 big-city police chiefs, is all the more disturbing when coupled with the *effects* of such discrepant executive behavior. When a chief fails to act in accordance with professed beliefs, he or she loses credibility. This loss of credibility is followed, inevitably, by a reduction in organizational effectiveness, efficiency, discipline, and employee morale. An erosion of public confidence in the police agency is a more or less certain consequence, as well. In a story all too familiar to America's big cities, the police chief, having lost credibility, is fired or pressured to resign or retire or the organization drags on for months or years under a weakened and dispirited form of leadership.

This publication describes the research on which these findings are based. It suggests that the structure of policing, and not the personalities of its chiefs, is at the heart of the problem. **Removing Managerial Barriers to Effective Police Leadership: A Study of Executive Leadership and Executive Management in Big-City Police Departments** calls for a major overhaul of the system—for a new model of executive leadership and management.

CONTENTS

LIST OF FIGURES

LIST OF TABLES

Chapter One

AN UNPARALLELED CHALLENGE TO POLICE LEADERSHIP

I know the police cause you trouble, but
they cause trouble everywhere. But when
you die and go to heaven there will be no
policemen there.

—"Hobo's Lullaby"
by Goebel Reeves

Big-city police work in the United States is steeped in a tradition of controversy. Even at its birth over 150 years ago, organized policing in the large urban centers of America was experienced as a thoroughly disreputable social institution. It was characterized by ineptitude, partisan politics, and a wide range of corrupt practices (Blumberg and Niederhoffer, 1985). And, while organized policing has moved, albeit often haltingly, through two waves of reform (Fogelson, 1977) and today enjoys substantial public support, it still faces what one observer aptly calls a "crisis of legitimacy" (Rumbaut, 1977). That crisis puts to the test the executive leadership of America's big-city police chiefs.

Additionally, danger, authority, emotional and physical fitness, cynicism, suspicion, affirmative action, budgetary limitations, and more all combine to place tremendous demands on the leadership of police executives (Geller, 1985).

Yet, as noted in Chapter Two, substantial evidence indicates that many chiefs exhibit a cautious and reactive orientation directed toward merely avoiding mistakes and maintaining the status quo. That orientation, rather than a more creative

1

approach to organizational leadership, works against not only the chiefs' success as leaders but also their professional survival.

The foregoing, along with other issues and problems described below, constitutes a crisis for big-city policing in America—a crisis that poses for police chief executive leadership a challenge unparalleled in the history of organized policing.

Difficulty of the Work

As police chief executives well realize, American police work is fraught with complexity and contradiction. Police officers are asked to confront crime and other community problems in a social milieu characterized by changing and conflicting service demands and enforcement priorities, as well as substantial—perhaps permanent—ambivalence about organized policing itself. Apart from disapprobation caused by abusive or neglectful police practices, Americans seem inherently resentful of the need for an organized police force, for such a visible and conspicuous authority-presence in their daily lives (Thompson and Stroud, 1984). Yet, in a nation that prides itself on its scientific, industrial, educational, and cultural achievements, this society has been forced to accept the reality of enormous lawlessness and the fear it engenders. Our society needs its police officers.

Tough But Dignified Service

In recent years, American society has experienced increases in stranger-on-stranger violence; a swelling of the ranks of lawless youth gangs; expansion and organization of the enormously profitable and dangerous illicit drug trade; an awakening to the reality of the wide scope and insidious nature of domestic violence, including spousal assault and child abuse; increased instances of bizarre, often drug-crazed, behavior; the proliferation of handguns; greater numbers of homeless people on the streets, more than a few of whom are a danger to themselves or to others; and a growing perception on the part of many that crime is out of control. Clearly, many Americans have changed the way they live because of their fear of crime (Wilson and Herrnstein, 1985; Silberman, 1978).

Americans want their police officers to be "tough on crime" but dignified in their treatment of citizens. And, while crime control is a high priority throughout the nation, many worry about the price of controlling crime and violence (Wilson and Herrnstein, 1985). What will it cost the nation, in dollars, to confront the crime problem? Will there be a move to sacrifice individual freedoms in the effort to achieve a safer and more civilized society? How does the society ensure that its officers are physically and emotionally tough enough and sufficiently self-disciplined to handle this difficult job sensitively and competently?

Support for the Officers

Police work often has profound effects on the people whose lives it touches, including, of course, those who do the work; yet support for higher standards and pay, better training, and more officers is often apparent only at times of crises in community-police relations or during highly publicized explosions in crime rates (Geller, 1985). Many officers properly look to the police chief for effective leadership in promoting the agency, its people, and their needs.

Police and Minorities

The police are often viewed with suspicion and mistrust in ethnic minority or economically disadvantaged communities, where the effects of patterned inequality and other social ills give rise to especially high rates of criminal violence and to a greater need for effective law enforcement. Establishing and maintaining effective community-police relations with all citizens is a critical responsibility of the agency's top executive, but it is an especially difficult job in those neighborhoods where the police are viewed as part of the crime problem (Klockars, 1985; Lipsky, 1970).

Organizational Structure: Barrier to Progress

The paramilitary bureaucratic structure of American law enforcement is intended to achieve organizational efficiency, control over the practices of individual officers, esprit de corps within the rank and file, and reasoned and responsible service to the community (Wilson and McLaren, 1972). It is apparently producing precisely the opposite results (Angell, 1973; Geller, 1985). Police chiefs in America are presiding over structures whose features function as formidable barriers to organizational effectiveness, communication, and morale, as well as a mutually satisfying relationship with the community.

Almost from the beginning, American policing has embraced a paramilitary bureaucratic organizational arrangement (Vollmer, 1936; Smith, 1940). Influenced by the principles of "scientific management" (Taylor, 1947), organized policing has been led by chief executives whose everyday work recognizes little or no distinction between leadership functions and managerial functions (Roberg, 1979). While the difference between the two functions may be of lesser significance in a small organization, it is believed to be critically important in a larger bureaucracy.

As Spencer (1971:126) noted, an "increase in mass is habitually accompanied by increase of structure" and of "differentiation." The inevitable increase in organizational

4

complexity that results from increases in size, structure, and differentiation of tasks, duties, and responsibilities suggests the strong likelihood that police chiefs will see themselves being forced to spend the bulk of their time in the managerial arena.

The managerial functions of an organization (those commonly associated with planning, organizing, directing, controlling, and the like) have long been respected and given extensive treatment in the literature and in organizational practice (most notably, Drucker, 1973). While much has been written on the subject, organizational leadership, on the other hand, has only recently begun to be addressed as a discipline separate and distinct from management (Burns, 1978; Bennis and Nanus, 1985; Block, 1987). Emerging in the literature and in the practices of a growing number of executives in the private sector is a deeply purposeful and "visionary" leadership orientation that differs dramatically from the traditional focus on "managing" an organization.

The time is ripe for an exploration of a more spirited and potentially more powerful form of leadership in big-city American policing, and for consideration of a new model of police administration, one that offers the potential for strengthening both executive leadership and executive management.

Policing's Past

American policing suffers both from its unenviable past and, ironically, from some of the very organizational mechanisms, such as the paramilitary structure, that have been introduced in the effort to reform the institution (Angell, 1973; Blumberg and Niederhoffer, 1985; Rumbaut and Bittner, 1979).

An examination of the early history of American law enforcement reveals deep-seated and pervasive problems of inefficiency, corruption, racism, brutality, and other forms of police lawlessness and discrimination (Blumberg and Niederhoffer, 1985). Further, organized policing has tended to align itself with power elites in most large cities across the country. Historically, the police have served the interests of the wealthy and powerful, often at the expense of those less fortunate (Balkan et al., 1980).

With the advent of mass communication, many Americans have been exposed, frequently in "real time," to the tendentiousness and the excesses of the police. In August 1968, for example, as the "whole world" watched on television, Chicago police rioted violently at the Democratic National Convention (National Commission on the Causes and Prevention of Violence, 1968).[*] Police relations with ethnic minorities, labor organizers, gays and lesbians, antiwar demonstrators, and other social activists have always been strained at best.

In what Fogelson (1977) described as "two waves" of police reform, responsible leadership in American law enforcement moved to curb abusive police practices. Those efforts, the first occurring around the turn of this century and the second beginning in the 1930s, achieved significant successes. The more obvious forms of institutionalized police corruption, for example, have been all but eliminated in most law enforcement agencies.

The vehicles of this reform were grounded in a civil service system, solidification and refinements in the paramilitary bureaucratic organizational arrangements, and the selection of "no-nonsense" police chiefs who ruled their agencies with an "iron fist" (Skolnick and Gray, 1975). While these mechanisms have had positive effects, they have also produced certain

---

[*]A more recent example that received widespread television coverage was the beating of motorist Rodney King in March 1991 by officers of the Los Angeles Police Department.

harmful results, the consequences of which function as an obstacle to continued reform efforts.

The principal problem with such mechanisms is that they ignore important structural and cultural dimensions of organizational life. With their reliance on technical and mechanistic approaches, they neglect the human and political realities of policing (Rumbaut, 1977). One effect of these early vehicles of reform is that they have imprisoned chiefs in an organizational arrangement that distances them from the communities they serve and from the needs, concerns, and aspirations of their own officers.

The "second wave" reforms, in particular, have created substantial barriers to effective communication within the organization, and they have, arguably, instilled a disrespect for truth and trust between the people who are hired to do police work and those who are promoted or appointed to lead it. Because such reforms have increased the social distance between the police chief and the cop on the beat, creating what Reuss-Ianni (1983) called the "two cultures of policing," it is virtually impossible for them to develop a common understanding of vital organizational and community needs.

The challenge, it may be argued, is to extend and expand the nascent efforts of a "third wave" of reform into a search for a more powerful form of police leadership, one that holds promise both for a deeper understanding of the reform issues and for substantial and lasting improvements in police service to the community.

Importance, Purpose, and Scope of the Study

Despite substantial progress in recent years, American policing still struggles for respect. Episodic instances of excessive force, criminal conduct, and other scandalous behavior characterize even the finest law enforcement agencies in the United

States. Many thousands of fine police officers labor under strained working conditions shaped only in part by conflicting community expectations and pressures, but mostly by the way they are treated by their own organizations. This study may have the effect of illuminating a new way of looking at police executive leadership and how it might be structured to meet the challenges of an effective, dignified, and satisfying police practice.

The purpose of this research was to determine how the values and behavior of America's big-city police chiefs can be identified and analyzed so that the contemporary challenge to police executive leadership might be more effectively met. The study explores the values of 52 police chiefs, what they stand for, and what they believe in, and it examines their leadership behavior as they carry out their executive functions in the workplace and in the community.

National in scope, the study sought to reveal answers to research questions (below) by examining the attitudes and executive behavior of police chiefs of large municipal law enforcement agencies throughout the country. The agencies are located in cities ranging in population from 208,000 to over 4.3 million.

Essentially a descriptive-comparative study, this research sought to answer the following specific questions:

1. What do America's big-city police chiefs profess to value in relation to their community and organizational responsibilities?

2. Is there a distinction in the relative importance the chiefs attach to executive *leadership* versus executive *management* functions or tasks?

3. Is the executive behavior of the police chiefs, as viewed by their immediate subordinates, consistent with their professed values?

4. Are there differences in the professed values or the observed behavior of the police chiefs based on individual or contextual demographic variables?

The study was designed to underscore a crucial distinction between the functions of executive leadership and executive management and to introduce a method by which police chiefs might be empowered to exercise a new, more purposeful, and more effective approach to leading and managing the police organization.

The theoretical foundation for this study is formed by the writings (explored in Chapter Two) of numerous researchers and observers in the fields of police administration, psychology, sociology, political science, and organizational leadership and management.

Chapter Two

TODAY'S LEADERSHIP CHALLENGE AS AN OUTGROWTH OF THE PAST

Chapter Two brings together the literature of American police administration and the more general literature of organizational leadership and management in an attempt to illustrate how past events and issues have shaped today's challenge to police executive leadership. In so doing, this chapter addresses the following areas: problems and challenges facing urban policing in America; concepts of organizational structure; concepts of organizational culture; functions and processes of leadership; the executive's role in the managerial process; effects of organizational structure and culture on executive leadership and management; and the link between police practices and leader behavior, including implications for change.

Problems and Challenges Facing Urban Policing in America

In 1931 the National Commission on Law Observance and Law Enforcement presented to President Hoover the results of its study of crime and justice in the United States (Blumberg and Niederhoffer, 1985). Known popularly as the Wickersham Commission, so named after its chairman, former U.S. Attorney General George W. Wickersham, the commission was highly critical of the everyday practices of American law enforcement. It cited, among many other ills, an insidious political spoils system and a complete lack of training as two of the root causes of police corruption, inefficiency, and brutality.

11

Some 57 years later, significant improvements have been made. Officer candidates are selected under, and protected by, a civil service merit system (More, 1981). Entry standards have been tightened and current-day screening includes an extensive background investigation and, in many parts of the country, psychological testing (Commission on Peace Officer Standards and Training, 1986; More, 1981). Extensive training is now required, and most of it conforms to standards set and controlled at the state level (Commission on Peace Officer Standards and Training, 1986; Goldstein, 1977). Technological advances, ranging from the two-way car radio to sophisticated computer applications in fiscal and personnel management and in crime fighting and service delivery, have taken place (Kelling et al., 1974). Finally, the quality of American police leadership has improved dramatically over the years (Geller, 1985).

Despite substantial progress, American policing still struggles for respect. There are, according to Blumberg and Niederhoffer, "amazing historical similarities in the relative permanence and continuity of the problems of the police as they confront the violent and disruptive episodes of every epoch" (1985:xi). Today, breaches of the public trust occur with sufficient frequency so that calls for police reform are fairly common in cities throughout the country; moreover, the apparent depth and range of the "police problem" suggest that "certain structural determinants and functions of the police role" operate to make police reform elusive, if not impossible (Rumbaut, 1977:6).

Policing's Early History

American cities, reacting to rampant crime problems brought on, in part, by the Industrial Revolution, sent representatives to London to examine the new British approach to police protection (Blumberg and Niederhoffer, 1985; Bouza,

1985; Skolnick and Gray, 1975; Smith, 1940). Organized police departments were soon created in Philadelphia (1833), Boston (1838), and New York (1844). By the 1870s, all large American cities had full-time police organizations (Bouza, 1985).

Unfortunately, the American systems were only crude approximations of the British approach to organized policing. Representatives of U.S. cities who traveled to London took note of the tall, smartly uniformed bobbies[*] and were impressed by their professional bearing. But, according to Skolnick and Gray (1975), the Americans neglected careful study of the historical foundations of the Metropolitan Police Act. Consequently, they failed to develop a thorough understanding of the risks associated with the creation of an organized police force.

From its earliest moments, municipal policing in America was attacked by citizens complaining of bribery, brutality, inefficiency, and a variety of other ills. Richardson (1970) described the process by which the New York Police Department was formed. He concluded that the corruption and other excesses found throughout the history of the organization may be traced to the failure of New York officials to consider the implications of an organized police force and to establish safeguards similar to those in England. He also made clear that local officials benefited personally from the absence of hiring standards and other safeguards. Klockars (1985) wrote that the process of becoming a 19th-century police officer in New York, Chicago, or other large eastern or midwestern city was quite simple: one simply went to the local ward leader or alderman with the customary sum of money.

---

[*]The imposing hat of the bobbies' uniform was created purposely to make the officers seem taller than the population they served.

Ironically, according to Klockars (1985), the organized police forces of both England and America were created not merely to attack more systematically the proliferating, often heinous crimes of the day. They were also created to curb the abuses of the various military, "watchman," and volunteer foot-patrol schemes of policing that had operated through the early 19th century. The plan was successful in England but not in the United States.

Two waves of reform. Having endured police abuses into the 1890s, "progressive elites" began what Fogelson (1977) called the first of two "waves" of police reform. The first wave, culminating in the Wickersham Commission report, was intended to wrest control of the police from the political machines in the nation's big cities. Civil service systems were established, along with a variety of other reforms. Fogelson suggested that these early reform efforts were generally successful, although limited in scope.

Another perspective, rare in the literature on police reform, is offered by Kelling (1985:304), who, while acknowledging the serious problems of early American policing, suggested that

> ...there are elements of exaggeration in this conventional characterization of early policing. The moral and political reformers (muckrakers, mugwumps, WASPs, and so on) had their own moral and political axes to grind and had real stakes in defining policing as they did. The picture was far more complex than many reformers would have us believe. Social work professionals were more than eager to portray police welfare practices in denigrating terms, not only to improve services but also to advance their own professional interests....There were chiefs who could and did resist venality. Likewise, there were officers who resisted corruption and political indebtedness....

During Fogelson's first wave of police reform, Raymond B. Fosdick found "a shifting leadership of mediocre calibre—varied now and then by flashes of real ability which are snuffed out when the political wheel turns" (Goldstein, 1977:380). Fosdick made this observation about police leadership in 1920. His view was supported by the Wickersham Commission (National Commission on Law Observance and Enforcement, 1968) when it identified incompetent agency leadership as the worst of the problems contributing to "police lawlessness."

The second wave of reform, Fogelson argued, began in the 1930s and continues to the present time. This movement was generated within the law enforcement community itself and is being advanced by today's city police departments.

Effects of the two waves of reform. By the 1960s substantial reform of important aspects of American policing had been accomplished. Civil service merit systems were firmly in place; rules and regulations prohibiting various types of unprofessional conduct had been written and communicated to officers; and blatant political interference, while still common in some major cities, had been significantly reduced throughout most of the country (President's Commission on Law Enforcement and the Administration of Justice, 1967).

In 1956 the California Peace Officers Research Association of California (PORAC) and the California Peace Officers Association (CPOA) wrote the nation's first law enforcement code of ethics (Bristow, 1975). The code was adopted a year later by the International Association of Chiefs of Police (IACP). It is now widely accepted as *the* code of ethics for the American police community. The statement expresses the officially espoused view of police leaders throughout the United States. (Other similar codes exist, such as the one of the National Sheriffs' Association.)

Even as police departments across the country were moving to adopt this inspiring code of ethics, serious new doubts were being expressed about the efficacy, the professional restraint, and, indeed, the very role of the country's police (Lipsky, 1970). As the nation moved from the calm of the 1950s into the socially turbulent 1960s, Americans were forced to confront *The Challenge of Crime in a Free Society* (a report by the President's Commission on Law Enforcement and Administration of Justice, published in 1967). Moreover, in their evaluation of the effectiveness of local police crime fighting, some Americans (Bittner, 1970; Chevigny, 1969; Clark, 1970; Cooper et al., 1975; Quinney, 1970) were beginning to question municipal policing's contribution to lawlessness in the community.

City Policing in the 1960s and 1970s

Many police observers were confident in the late 1950s and early 1960s that the institution of municipal policing had finally gained a measure of long-pursued respectability (Carte and Carte, 1975). They attributed this perceived increase in public confidence to the pioneering efforts of people like O. W. Wilson, superintendent of police in Chicago; William Parker, police chief in Los Angeles; and, of course, August Vollmer. Lesser known chiefs, such as Clarence Kelley of Kansas City, Missouri, and Elmer Jansen of San Diego, California, also contributed to Fogelson's (1977) second wave of police reform in the United States. These were "no-nonsense" chief executives who, during the 1940s, 1950s, and early part of the 1960s, did much to rid their organizations of the more obvious forms of corruption, including bribery, extortion, and the acceptance of gratuities. That some of this progress was illusory will be made clear later.

Because of their belief that the public had come to respect both their reform efforts and the results, these chiefs—and their successors—were shocked when, beginning in the mid-1960s, city police in America came under unprecedented attack.

Crime, politics, and the police. One of the reasons for this attack, noted earlier, was that Americans tend to believe that the police are responsible for controlling crime, and crime was clearly on the increase during the 1960s and 1970s (Silberman, 1978; Stamper et al., 1981). Furthermore, because of increasing pressures to reduce crime, some police departments began to manipulate crime statistics (Clark, 1970). As evidence of this practice was exposed, doubts about police efficiency and integrity grew.

Often neglected in discussions of crime rates and police practices is the fundamentally political nature of all aspects of police work. Quinney (1975), for example, argues that crime rates are "political devices," manipulated by police departments and politicians to meet their budgetary and political ends. There is no reason to believe that such manipulations were uncommon prior to the 1960s. It is reasonable to conclude, however, that broader public awareness of such practices during the 1960s contributed to an increasing cynicism about the police (Clark, 1970; Goldstein, 1977).

To complicate matters, society, including its half million police officers, was engaged in a spirited national debate over the effects of U.S. Supreme Court decisions in the arena of the criminal law. The Warren era introduced significant restrictions on police practices, with the *Miranda* decision on confessions producing the greatest controversy (Blumberg and Niederhoffer, 1985). The public's fear of crime, combined with doubts about certain police practices, made taking sides a discomfiting proposition for those who believed in both crime control and the tenets of due process of law.

National politics and local police. By 1968, however, the "law and order" campaign of Richard Nixon had helped to make clear the lines between police supporters and police critics. Rioting in black ghettos, antiwar demonstrations, and occasional skirmishes with hippies at "love-ins" and other "happenings" had brought police-community relations issues into sharp focus (Balkan et al., 1980). Combined with a dramatic increase in predatory street crimes—robbery, criminal homicide, burglary, rape, auto theft, and the like (Silberman, 1978)—the nation appeared divided about its police forces.

Then, in August 1968, the Chicago Police Department rioted on national television (National Commission on the Causes and Prevention of Violence, 1968). Responsible for maintaining order at the Democratic National Convention that year, the police, encouraged by Mayor Richard J. Daley, engaged in a pattern of violent, unlawful behavior (1968:i):

> On the part of the police there was enough wild club swinging, enough cries of hatred, enough gratuitous beating, to make the conclusion inescapable that individual policemen, and lots of them, committed violent acts far in excess of the requisite force for crowd dispersal or arrest....

> Although the crowds were finally dispersed on the nights of violence, the problems they represent have not been. Surely this is not the last time a...dissenting group will clash with those whose duty it is to enforce the law. And the next time the whole world will be watching.

Chevigny (1969:280) suggested that, for many Americans, the police actions in Chicago were understandable, even acceptable. He argued that the "police have become the repository of all the illiberal impulses in this liberal society; they are under heavy fire because most of us no longer admit so readily to our illiberal impulses as we once did."

Others (Balkan et al., 1980; Bayley and Mendelsohn, 1968; Quinney, 1970, 1975) echoed this sentiment and expanded upon it when they argued that the police are "used" by those in power. In explaining, for example, why they do not welcome larger American police forces as a "step toward a safer and more decent society," Cooper and colleagues (1975:8) stated

> The answer lies in our basic view of the functions that the police perform in the United States today, and have performed throughout United States history. Although the actual role of the police at any given time—like the role of the state in general or advanced capitalist societies—is complex and should not be oversimplified, it is clear that the police have *primarily* served to enforce the class, racial, sexual, cultural oppression that has been an integral part of the development of capitalism in the U.S.

Balkan, Berger, and Schmidt (1980:101) offered support for this view, suggesting that local police were "incapable of containing the violence" of the "political and economic conflict over the Vietnam War, the civil rights movement, [and] severe rebellions by the black and poor," in part, because "through overly brutal and ineffective methods, they seemed to contribute to the decline of legitimacy and stability of the system."

According to Bayley and Mendelsohn (1968:172–173), "Americans, it is fair to say, are in the process of making up their minds about the kinds of policies police departments should implement toward minority groups."

Other effects of the "second wave" of police reform. The social upheaval of the 1960s and 1970s and the police role in all of it produced several significant studies: The American Bar Association's *Standards Relating to the Urban Police Function* (1973); *The Challenge of Crime in a Free Society: A Report* by the President's Commission on Law Enforcement and Administration of Justice (1967); *The Knapp Commission Report on Police Corruption* (published in 1973, detailing corruption within the New York Police Department); the National Advisory Commission on Criminal Justice Standards and Goals report (1973); and the National Commission on the Causes and Prevention of Violence report (1968). What is clear from each of these studies is that America's police forces were in great need of a "third wave" of substantive political and organizational reform just 20 years ago.

The "Third Wave" of Police Reform

In response to numerous recommendations to strengthen its crime-fighting capabilities, improve relations with the community, and rid itself of incompetent, apathetic, and brutal police officers, the American institution of policing began in the early 1970s what appeared to be a significant, albeit fragmented, process of role transformation and reform (Blumberg and Niederhoffer, 1985; Goldstein, 1977; Skolnick and Gray, 1975).

The Police Foundation. Leading the way was the Police Foundation, in Washington, D.C. Funded by the Ford Foundation in 1970, the Police Foundation sought out local police departments with chiefs who were willing to challenge traditional police practices. The Foundation found such departments in Kansas City, Missouri, in Dayton and Cincinnati,

20

Ohio, in San Diego, California, and in several other cities. In Kansas City, for example, the attitude of Chief Clarence Kelley was expressed succinctly in 1971: "Many of us in the department had the feeling we were training, equipping, and deploying men to do a job neither we, nor anyone else, knew much about" (Kelling et al., 1974:i).

Supporting institutions. The "third wave" reforms have been aided by the creation of the Police Executive Research Forum (PERF). Consisting of approximately 540 U.S. law enforcement chief executives, and supported by a large "subscribing" membership of leading criminal justice practitioners and retired chiefs, PERF is characterized by the qualifications it imposes on its members. All must be college graduates, committed to research, willing to develop and implement standards[*] for improvement of the law enforcement field, and subscribe to the "principles embodied in the Constitution" as the foundation of American policing (Geller, 1985). Collectively, PERF members serve more than 30 percent of the nation's population.

In California the state's Commission on Peace Officer Standards and Training (POST) has taken great strides to further the professionalization of police work (Commission on Peace Officer Standards and Training, 1986). It sponsors courses in basic and intermediate police training, executive development, middle management, and basic supervision. POST uses a certification process based on successful completion of these courses. POST certification is now being used in the promotional processes of most California police departments. In

---

*The program is not intended to serve as a substitute for a higher education in the state's college and university systems. POST officials see it as a means of enriching the education of police leaders, most of whom have already been awarded bachelor's or master's degrees.

addition, the agency created a "command college" in 1984 that offers police executives the equivalent of a master's degree[*] in police leadership and administration. The command college has a strong "futures" orientation, encouraging its students to study a wide range of issues that will affect policing in the years ahead.

Problems persist. Still, problems persist. As noted previously (Blumberg and Niederhoffer, 1985:xi), "amazing historical similarities in the relative permanence and continuity of the problems of the police" continue to plague municipal law enforcement. Moore and Kelling (1983) were disturbed that, despite all that has been done to improve both the effectiveness and the image of local policing, the "professionalism" movement has not been more successful. Municipal policing, they argued, is cleaner, faster, and more efficient, but its drawbacks are even more obvious today. Moore and Kelling see the police as at least as isolated and disengaged from the communities they serve as they were 30 years ago. They are not alone in the belief that much more needs to be done to improve police effectiveness and police-community relations (Andrews, 1985; Blumberg and Niederhoffer, 1985; Brown, 1985; Fyfe, 1985; Geller, 1985; Iannone, 1987; Kerstetter, 1985; Klockars, 1985; Langworthy, 1986; Mayo, 1985; Punch, 1985; Sherman, 1985; Skolnick and Bayley, 1986; Walker, 1985; Williams, 1985). Many believe that not until police officers themselves perceive a need for improvement will policing achieve significant and lasting reform.

---

*PERF is one of the founders of the Commission on Accreditation for Law Enforcement Agencies, whose professional standards have been adopted by numerous law enforcement agencies in the United States and elsewhere.

The Police Culture: View From the Streets

> I guess what our job really boils down to is
> not letting the assholes take over the city.
> Now I'm not talking about your regular
> crooks...they're bound to wind up in the
> joint anyway. What I'm talking about are
> those shitheads out to prove they can push
> everybody around. Those are the assholes
> we gotta deal with and take care of on
> patrol....They're the ones that make it
> tough on the decent people out there. You
> take the majority of what we do and it's
> nothing more than asshole control. (Man-
> ning and Van Maanen, 1978:221)

This view by a veteran police officer is fairly typical of
statements expressed by many officers whose work has been
studied by police ethnographers and other researchers (Alex,
1969; Berkley, 1969; Droge, 1973; Leinen, 1984; Maas, 1973;
McClure, 1984; Muir, 1977; Rumbaut, 1977; Terkel, 1975;
Westley, 1970; Whittemore, 1969). Adding considerable
weight to the evidence that many of America's police officers
have an essentially negative or cynical view of society—and
their role in it—is the work of police officers who have moved
into writing careers, either as journalists (T. Walker, 1969) or
as novelists (Wambaugh, 1970, 1972).

The work. The vivid accounts of these researchers and
writers offer fascinating, often disturbing, insights into the
work of America's big-city police. Terkel (1975), for example, captured the flavor of a young New York police officer
who is assigned to emergency service. The officer talks about
his experiences with "jumpers," "floaters," and other suicide
victims, including maggot-infested "hangers." As a new
father, the officer is exposed regularly to child abuse, other
domestic violence, and crib deaths. Snipers, some recently

23

returned from Vietnam, fire upon him and his colleagues as they go about their work. His world is dangerous, often noxious, and, by any standard, emotionally traumatic.

But as noted throughout the literature—and confirmed by this researcher's 22 years in police work—many officers do not express directly their emotional reactions to these experiences. Terkel's New York officer, for example, while fearing that he was moving toward a "feelingless" state, nonetheless talked about the need to maintain control at all times. One simply cannot get sick at the scene of a gruesome automobile crash, industrial accident, homicide, or suicide.

Authority and danger: Constituents of the police culture. Skolnick (1966) wrote that the authority and self-perceived *danger* inherent in police work combine to create a powerful police culture, the most obvious features of which are (1) a common world view that reflects a basic suspicion of those who are outside police work and who, consequently, do not understand its pressures and (2) a powerful solidarity among street cops. His contention was that police officers develop a "we-they" attitude that precludes the development of effective police-community relations.

Police cynicism. Arthur Niederhoffer, a former New York city police lieutenant who became a sociologist and criminologist, argued on the basis of considerable research (1969) that people of widely varying motives become police officers. Common to most, however, is some degree of commitment to the idea of "helping others." Exposed to a remarkably strong acculturation process, the new officer soon leaves behind—either temporarily or permanently—large parts of his or her pre-existing value and belief systems.

Niederhoffer posited a "cynicism" theory that argues that an individual's cynicism builds quickly once the officer is assigned to the field and exposed to "real world" experiences

24

and, most significantly, to the "processing" of those experiences by and with senior officers. The causes are the same in all areas of the country (Clark, 1970; Maas, 1973; Skolnick and Gray, 1975). New officers witness countless examples of "man's inhumanity to man"; injustices in the justice system; nonpolice friends and family members who do not comprehend the nature of police work and its unique pressures; an unfriendly press; and a perceived lack of support from the public and their bosses, both within the department and in city hall. Westley (1970) believed that many officers come to view the public as their enemy.

Stages of an officer's career. Niederhoffer (from Blumberg and Niederhoffer, 1985:209) developed a model that reflected his view of the stages of an officer's career in law enforcement. His research suggested that cynicism peaks between the officer's fifth and tenth year; the model, reprinted here as *Figure 2-1*, makes clear the importance of how an officer deals with his or her cynicism.

Figure 2-1
Niederhoffer's Cynicism Development Theory
Typical Stages of a Police Officer's Career:
From Commitment to Anomie

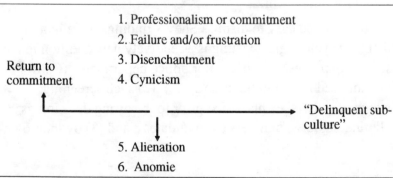

1. Professionalism or commitment
2. Failure and/or frustration
3. Disenchantment
4. Cynicism

Return to commitment

"Delinquent subculture"

5. Alienation
6. Anomie

Source: Blumberg and Niederhoffer, 1985
Reprinted with permission from Niederhoffer, Arthur. *Behind the Shield: Police in Urban Society*. Doubleday.

Niederhoffer distinguished between "pseudo-cynicism" of the type often found in police academy training, "romantic cynicism" common during the first five years on the job, and "aggressive cynicism," which "depends on the conjunction of individual cynicism and the subculture of cynicism" (Blumberg and Niederhoffer, 1985:209). According to his model, that point at which romantic cynicism begins to flag is crucial. If, through whatever means, the officer is directed back toward a "return to commitment," it bodes well, both for the individual (Stamper, 1986) and for the community. If, on the other hand, the cynic becomes "increasingly pessimistic," his or her cynicism may lead to a "passive" or "apathetic" attitude, expressing itself "as a form of mellow if mild good will. It accepts and comes to terms with the flaws of the system" (Blumberg and Niederhoffer, 1985:209). Far worse is the cynical police officer whose misanthropic cynicism leads to psychological anomie, aggression toward or virtually total withdrawal from family and community, and the distinct possibility of suicide.

"Good cops/bad cops." In a controversial book, *Good Cops/Bad Cops,* Shev and Hewes (1977) argued that roughly a third of all American police officers are psychologically unsuited for police work.

It would be easy to dismiss Shev's findings were it not true that (1) psychological testing is a relatively new addition to the screening process of most major police departments (California imposed its requirement in 1982); (2) such screening, which usually takes place just prior to the hiring decision, is eliminating large numbers of candidates[*]; and (3) by their own

---

*Up to 60 percent of all candidates who survive the screening process, prior to psychological testing, are subsequently rejected by the department psychologist in the San Diego Police Department.

admission, many big-city police chiefs acknowledge the presence in their ranks of people unsuited to the work.

Equal employment opportunity. The nationwide effort to make municipal police departments representative of the communities they serve has posed a significant challenge to law enforcement. Across the country, women and ethnic minorities, often aided by consent decrees or court orders, have been finding jobs, preferred assignments, and promotions in city police departments, long the exclusive domain of white males. The struggle has been characterized by resistance ranging from "cold shoulder" treatment to outright defiance and, in a few instances, to violence between and among police officers (Alex, 1969; Lord, 1983; Leinen, 1984; Milton, 1972).

The Leadership Challenge

> "Democracy is always hard on the police,"
> bemoaned senior patrolman Altifuchs....
> "During the Nazi period, Goring said,
> 'When a policeman shoots, I shoot.' That
> made everything clear. A policeman knew
> where he stood and what he was expected
> to do...."
>
> —Berkley, 1969:1

Reuss-Ianni (1983) suggested that there are "two cultures of policing": the culture of the "street cop" and the culture of the "management cop." Much of the literature supports the notion of a significant and growing cultural gap, accompanied by an estrangement, between police administrators and their officers (Bouza, 1985; Fogelson, 1977; Geller, 1985; Skolnick, 1966). This gap offers a clear picture of the leadership challenge for the American police chief executive.

Ideologies of policing. Lauer (1982:182) defined ideologies as "legitimation of a particular order; they arise out of that order, and they tend to perpetuate it by adorning it with

27

legitimacy." While police chiefs and police officers may belong to the same organization, the same infrastructure of the municipal government, and, in some instances, even the same employee association, their ideologies are often strikingly different and frequently in direct conflict with each other (Berkley, 1969; Reuss-Ianni, 1983; Stamper, 1976, 1977). There is ample evidence, for example, that police administrators and police officers may view the roles and responsibilities of law enforcement in fundamentally different ways (Adams et al., 1985; Bouza, 1985; Brown, 1985).

One explanation (Andrews, 1985:5) for such significant differences in ideology between those who do police work and those who lead it may be found in a web of contradictions surrounding the work itself:

> Few municipal functions are simultaneously as sensitive to the citizenry, as routine and as unpredictable, as rule-bound and as discretionary, as supervised by external oversight and as unsupervised (even invisible) in daily detail as is policing. And no other city function is so likely to touch the lives of any citizen as unexpectedly or in such unpleasant circumstances.

While differences between management and labor exist everywhere, in few occupations do these differences seem to carry the significance they do in policing. The work of the cop on the beat and the work of the chief in the office can be worlds apart, and the consequences of failing to understand each other's world can be grave (Adams et al., 1985). Crime fighting, service delivery, police-community relations, officer safety, equal employment opportunity and other personnel practices, and employee morale—all may suffer because of a lack of mutual understanding within the organization (Geller, 1985; Officer Safety Task Force Report, 1985; Stamper, 1977).

28

Police chief executives are well aware that the average tenure of big-city chiefs has been placed at a mere 2.8 years (Geller, 1985).[*] Frequently, the reasons for such short-lived careers are found in the conduct of individual officers whose behavior has produced "unpleasant circumstances." Controversial police shootings and unethical or criminal conduct, especially when combined with escalating crime rates and eroding public confidence, offer the greatest risk to the occupational survival of the chief executive (Fyfe, 1985; Geller, 1985; Hudnut, 1985; Iannone, 1987; Kerstetter, 1985; *The Knapp Commission Report on Police Corruption*, 1973; Leonard and More, 1971; Mayo, 1985; Punch, 1983, 1985; Scott, 1986; Skousen, 1977; Walker, 1985; Wilson and McLaren, 1972).

In an effort to prevent police abuses, many chief executives exhibit what might be called a "control" ideology, their principal purpose being *avoidance* of poor performance and officer misconduct rather than *pursuit* of excellent performance and ethical conduct (Berkley, 1969; Geller, 1985). Schein (1985) distinguished between these two orientations by labeling the former "anxiety avoidance" and the latter "positive problem-solving." The behavior of two individuals with opposite orientations may be identical, but the motive base is entirely different and, according to Schein, individuals with the anxiety avoidance orientation react out of "feelings of dread (of being threatened from known or unknown sources) and varying degrees of cognitive disorientation (of not knowing what is going on or what is ahead)" (1985:177).

---

*This study offers evidence that average tenure has increased since the 1976 survey that Geller describes. As noted in Chapter Four, the tenure of chiefs now averages 4.1 years. However, since Geller does not define "big-city," it is not possible to know whether this comparison is valid.

Clearly, the personal orientation or ideology of the police chief executive is a critical variable in the executive's capacity to meet the leadership challenge—to prevent, anticipate, and solve problems.

Police discretion. A crucible for the police administrator is his or her ability to define and manage the enormous discretionary decision-making power of individual police officers (Davis, 1971). Few people seem to realize either the breadth or the necessity of police discretion. Indeed, most Americans, according to Quinney (1970), fail to see that the essence of effective policing is to be found in the judicious exercise of individual decision making. Discretion is the "principal characteristic of law enforcement," yet "there is...a generalized public feeling that since discretion involves personal decisions on the part of police, the operation of such discretion is totally improper in a democratic society" (Quinney, 1970:105). From the communications dispatcher to the officer on the beat, critical *choices* are made on a daily basis: to send a car or not, to stop a suspicious person or not, to write a traffic citation or not, to arrest or not, to shoot or not.

Ironically, unlike many other professions, the level of discretion in police work and the immediate consequences of its use are far greater at the bottom of the organization than at the top (Davis, 1971). The challenge for the police chief executive, then, is to set and enforce sensible limitations and guidelines for the exercise of the enormous discretionary power of those at the operational level of the organization (American Bar Association, 1973; Davis, 1971; Goldstein, 1975, 1977).

Resource appropriation, allocation, and distribution. How many police officers are needed to police a city effectively and efficiently? How many support personnel are needed? How many supervisors and managers are needed to ensure that leadership and managerial responsibilities are met? What other forms of support (training, supplies, equipment, and the like) are necessary? Those are the kinds of questions that occupy much of the executive's time (Drucker, 1973; Fyfe, 1985; Langworthy, 1986; Mintzberg, 1980; Munro, 1974; Roberg, 1979; Scott, 1986; Swanson and Territo, 1983; Weber, 1946; Williamson, 1984; Wilson and McLaren, 1972).

The police chief executive is responsible for developing the basic budget or appropriations request (Wilson and McLaren, 1972). What the executive wants may not be, and usually is not, what the city manager or city council or mayor is willing or able to provide. This reality makes clear the need for the police executive to develop solid political skills and effective relationships with key people in city government. Making that challenge even greater is the need for the police chief to understand and appreciate overall priorities of local government and, given the style of his or her boss, to perform as an integral part of the city's team of department heads (Garmire, 1982; Wilson and McLaren, 1972).

The method of competing or negotiating for resources varies widely throughout the country (Geller, 1985). In some cities, the process is openly political. In others, the budgetary process is more "professional," with severe restrictions imposed on the police chief. This is most often the case in cities with appointed, rather than elected, chiefs; since the vast majority of police chiefs are appointed (either by the mayor or the city manager, usually subject to city council confirmation), the need for strong political and interpersonal skills is apparent (Garmire, 1982).

The allocation and the distribution of resources, while still influenced to varying degrees by the larger political process, offer an opportunity for the police chief to establish the organization's priorities (Wilson and McLaren, 1972). How many officers will be allocated, for example, to patrol work, to investigative work? How, within those assignments, will personnel be distributed or deployed? Given the results of recent experimentation (Brown, 1986; Kelling, 1974; Rumbaut and Stamper, 1974; Shapard, 1985; Skolnick and Bayley, 1986; Sweeney and Ellingsworth, 1973), the police chief faces significant challenges in answering these questions. Traditional practices, as noted earlier, may or may not represent a wise investment of organizational resources. Former commissioner of the New York City Police Department, Patrick Murphy, for instance, attacked the considerably expensive practice of preventive patrol as "aimless": "Its major purpose seems to be to reassure the citizen that the police department, like the city zoo, exists" (Silberman, 1978:207).

No matter how it is approached, resource allocation and distribution will signal both to the community and to the organization's employees what the chief executive values. It will communicate, for example, the relative importance of patrol work versus investigative work, of child abuse versus burglary investigations, of the work of sworn versus nonsworn members of the department.

Political independence of the department. A large number of writers have commented upon the exploitation or the misuse of police power by wealthy or otherwise powerful influences in the community (American Bar Association, 1973; Balkan et al., 1980; Chevigny, 1969; Cooper et al., 1975; Goldstein, 1975; Hudnut, 1985; Lipsky, 1970; Moore and Kelling, 1983; Murphy, 1985; Quinney, 1970, 1975; Reiss, 1971, 1985; Rubenstein, 1973; Scott, 1986; Sklonick, 1966; Toch et al., 1975; S. Walker, 1985). These writers, with widely differing political perspectives, have witnessed in the history of American law enforcement the tendency of the police to be pulled out of their constitutionally mandated position of "nonalignment." That is, the police have not always been neutral in situations where neutrality is both required and expected.

Throughout its history, the institution of policing has been manipulated, to varying degrees, by the economically and politically powerful, such that it has been relatively easy to discern whose interests the local police department is serving. For example, historically, the police have been aligned with management in labor strife, with merchants over consumers, with landlords over tenants. Numerous commissions, as noted previously, have condemned the police for "taking sides" in, if not actually initiating, race riots and violent disruptions of antiwar and other political demonstrations.

This tendency to become "aligned," when a studied and professional neutrality by the police is most needed, is facilitated when the police chief executive is not politically independent. Andrews (1985) argued forcefully for structuring the political independence of the police chief. He is supported by Fraser (1985), Hudnut (1985), and Murphy (1985); the latter urged city police chiefs and mayors to "negotiate" the limits of such independence, to develop a clear understanding of roles and responsibilities, and to ensure that the police chief is kept an arm's distance from any and all political entanglements.

Corruption and brutality. A single act of corruption or brutality can do serious, perhaps lasting, damage to the reputation of the police organization. Since public confidence and support are essential to effective and efficient policing (Brown, 1985; Moore and Kelling, 1983), the police chief must be intimately familiar with the causes and prevention of such behavior (Blumberg and Niederhoffer, 1985; Goldstein, 1975; Kerstetter, 1985). Accordingly, the chief must set and enforce reasonable, job-related, and nondiscriminatory standards of performance and conduct for all police employees. Standards relating especially to ethics, integrity, and treatment of the public must be viewed and understood as *nonnegotiable* (Stamper, 1977).

According to each of the national commissions cited previously, virtually all of the agency's personnel processes need to reflect this concern for professional police practices, recruitment, candidate screening, entry-level education and training, performance evaluation and other supervisory practices, career development programs, promotions and other incentives, and, of course, the system of employee discipline.

Internal versus external controls. The issue of internal versus external control of America's police has been debated for years, with the argument usually centering around "civilian review boards" (American Bar Association, 1973; Carte and Carte, 1975; Chevigny, 1969; Cooper et al., 1975; Goldstein, 1975; Kerstetter, 1985; Lipsky, 1970; Punch, 1983, 1985; S. Walker, 1985; Williams, 1985). The chief executive, regardless of the model of review—internal or external—has ultimate responsibility for establishing and maintaining discipline within the police department. Handled credibly, this one responsibility can do more for the image and reputation of the agency than any other executive function (Geller, 1985). Yet, as Punch (1985), the United States Congress (1984), and Yates (1985) have illustrated, police corruption, in particular, has been remarkably resistant to elimination.

In the pursuit of more effective solutions, Schmidt (1985) envisioned an expansion of police malpractice litigation, with greater resort to the use of 42 U.S. Code, section 1983, which prohibits civil rights violations under color of state law.

In the most sensitive area of police force, that of deadly force, the American Bar Association (1973) urged police chiefs to "effectively market" controlling policies on the use of firearms, not just to the public but to police officers as well.

34

Labor relations. In a comprehensive article on the police labor movement in the United States, Bouza raised the question "Police Unions: Paper Tigers or Roaring Lions?" He concluded that while most police officers are "cops first" and only secondarily union members, "We have seen that given the proper issues, the cops can be radicalized and galvanized to furious and effective actions" (1985:279). Bouza cautioned against police executives "poaching on labor's legitimate preserves," but he also argued strongly for the development of competent managers to help avoid the kinds of problems that can turn police officers into "roaring lions."

Problems that can erupt into significant police labor disputes must include, of course, wages, hours, and terms and conditions of employment (Bouza, 1985). But other delicate issues, perceived or real, must be tended carefully by the chief executive: violations of due process in investigating or disciplining officers; policies, procedures, or equipment that jeopardize the safety of police officers; restriction of the right to engage in lawful political activities; unfair or unwise promotional processes; quotes in the media that reflect inaccurately or unfairly on the performance or conduct of employees; and, generally, a lack of sensitivity to the work force.

In addition to police management and the police unions and employee associations themselves, disparate forces in the community seek either to restrict the growth of police unionism or to expand or protect the rights of police officers. What makes this curious to those with a narrow view of the issues is that some liberals (Juris, 1971) are advocates of greater restrictions on police rights while others—the American Civil Liberties Union, for example—publish books on and advocate strongly for police officer rights (Brancato and Polebaum, 1981). Most civil libertarians would argue that these positions are not mutually exclusive at all, drawing an analogy from the criminal justice system itself: any apparent contradictions are in the eye of those who mistakenly perceive respect for "due process" and respect for "crime control" as irreconcilable polar extremes. Angell (1973) and Berkley (1969) argued that the expansion of police officers' rights, and, indeed the "democratization" of America's police departments, would have the effect of increasing individual officers' sense of responsibility for their own behavior.

The chief's presentation of self. Goffman, in his classic work (1959), argued that individuals present themselves differently depending on their situation. The police chief executive moves regularly from one "stage" to another, performing essentially the same role but with different emphases: as head of a large municipal bureaucracy and member of the city's management team; as leader of a police executive staff; as the city's "top cop"; and as the department's premier ambassador to the community and to the rank and file. Occasionally, the chief executive performs several of these roles simultaneously on the same stage. Even apart from the complexity added when the executive's *personal* roles (as parent, spouse, coach, PTA president) are taken into consideration, the challenge is as formidable as it is clear: the police chief must, under extraordinary pressure, be an effective *manager of self* (Bennis and Nanus, 1985).

Several contributors to the police literature (Mayo, 1985; Reiss, 1985; Scott, 1986; Skolnick and McCoy, 1985; Skousen, 1977) offered concrete suggestions to assist the chief executive in combining substance and image in ways that are intended to ensure at least survival, if not success.

Sherman advanced the argument that the American police chief ought to become a "statesman," by which he means "a leader of a democracy, someone who can transcend the current values of the day and lead both police and the public into

36

accepting a better set of values and strategies for policing"
(1985:462). He argued that

> Any movement for professionalizing police manage-
> ment needs a constant dialectic between expertise and
> accountability, between professional standards for re-
> search and public demands. Professionals are very
> good at adapting their practices to the examples of a
> few statesmanlike leaders. But without that leadership,
> it is unlikely that policing can be substantially im-
> proved.

Concepts of Organizational Structure

Municipal law enforcement in the United States has been
organized essentially along paramilitary-bureaucratic lines
since its inception (Fosdick, 1969; Smith, 1940). According to
Berkley (1969), Bittner (1970), and Munro (1974), these organizational arrangements have had profound effects both on
the nature and quality of police-community relations and on
the nature and quality of organizational life. Only a few
writers, most prominently Skousen (1977) and Wilson and
McLaren (1972), favored the retention of existing organizational arrangements. At least one writer, while maintaining respect
for the power of the structure, tended to minimize its importance as a determinant of police behavior (Langworthy, 1986).
Most theorists, however, argue that the paramilitary bureaucratic structure frustrates the reform efforts of progressive
police chief executives.

Bureaucracy

Bureaucracy—the term has a distinctly pejorative connota-
tion in many circles. Block (1987:191) wrote, for example,
"The essence of bureaucracy is never to get excited about anything." Max Weber (1946:215), often described as the
progenitor of the bureaucratic concept, reinforced that view:

"The 'objective' discharge of business primarily means a discharge of business according to *calculable rules* and 'without regard for persons.' " That impersonal approach to organizational life is, in fact, the essence of bureaucracy, according to Weber. Organizational complexity is best managed, according to Weber (1946:215), with "[b]ureaucratization [that] offers above all the optimum possibility for carrying through the principle of specializing administrative functions according to purely objective considerations."

According to the studies of Hsu and Marsh (1983) "functional specialization" and "knowledge complexity," both nurtured by bureaucratic organizations, are significant sources of organizational power (the exercise of which is typically evaluated in value-laden terms both by the power-wielding incumbents and by those they influence).

Many critics of bureaucracy continue to see it as an essential mechanism for the organization and accomplishment of important work; their criticism is aimed at making bureaucracy more effective and more responsive to those who rely on bureaucratic work for goods, services, gainful employment, or professional satisfaction.

The Police Paramilitary Bureaucracy

> There is a need, right now, for extensive structural reorganization of some of the largest and most important of our police establishments, for provision of more effective means for assuring popular control, further development of various central services in order to effect a closer coordination of widely dispersed police activities, improved procedures for recruitment, training, promotion and discipline, and for the advancement of professional standards generally. (Smith, 1940:xxiii)

38

Smith's message was heeded. It was during Fogelson's (1977) "second wave" of police reform, beginning in the 1930s and lasting until the 1960s, that American police departments underwent "extensive structural reorganization," following generally the pattern of American business and industry, and borrowing as well from the military. Centralization and specialization, in particular, were adopted to meet a variety of needs associated with increasing size, complexity, and control (Garmire, 1982; Wilson and McLaren, 1972).

This rather massive reorganization effort was guided by the works of Frederick Taylor (1947), August Vollmer (1936), O. W. Wilson (Wilson and McLaren, 1972), whose original *Police Administration* was published in 1950, and, of course, Max Weber (1946). According to Leonard and More (1971), Vollmer wrote survey-and-reorganization reports as a consultant to the police departments in Dallas, Texas (1944); Havana, Cuba (1929); Kansas City, Missouri (1928); Los Angeles, California (1925); Minneapolis, Minnesota (1930); Syracuse, New York (1944); and Portland, Oregon (1947). O. W. Wilson did the same in Hartford, Connecticut (1942); Greensboro, North Carolina (1941); Pasadena, California (1940); San Antonio, Texas (1933); and Wichita, Kansas (1930).

Manifestations of the paramilitary model. From the beginning, as noted, policing in the United States has been organized along paramilitary lines (Fosdick, 1969; Smith, 1940). *Webster's New Collegiate Dictionary* (1979) defines "paramilitary" as "formed on a military pattern...." Embracing such basic principles as unity of command and span of control, large American police departments follow the military pattern, using titles such as "sergeant," "lieutenant," "captain," and "commander." Most West Coast agencies eschew the use of military titles for their highest ranks. Departments are headed by "chiefs," "assistant chiefs," and "deputy chiefs." In parts of the East and the Midwest, police departments may be headed by "commissioners" and "superintendents." But in other cities, Kansas City, Missouri, for example, police departments are headed by "colonels," "lieutenant colonels," and "majors."

There are other manifestations of the paramilitary orientation. One, of course, is the quasimilitary uniform of the patrol or traffic officer. The rules and regulations of most police departments make clear the expectation that nonranking officers will exhibit deference toward ranking officers; saluting, while rare in California, is not uncommon in some other jurisdictions, especially on ceremonial occasions. New officers are "recruits" or "cadets," and spend part of their academy time marching in formation from class to class. Sergeants head "squads" and work under a "platoon" system.

Scientific management and paramilitary organization. It is the confluence of the paramilitary and "scientific management" orientations that has led one scholar to refer to American police officers as "soldier bureaucrats" (Bittner, 1970). The conditions created by the intersection of these two orientations might also give rise to concerns resulting from the work of Milgram (1974) on authority. For example, does the structure of American law enforcement, combined perhaps with Skolnick's (1966) "danger-authority" theory of police behavior, foster an attitude of "blind obedience" in sensitive situations where independence and maturity are required?

As noted previously, an important distinguishing characteristic of police departments is that the people at the bottom of the organizational hierarchy—the police officers—have enormous discretionary decision-making power. This reality, combined with an increasing awareness of the effects of autocratic rule and binding organizational structures, is causing many writers to question the appropriateness of the paramilitary model for police work (Angell, 1973; Berkley, 1969; Bittner,

1970; Blumberg and Niederhoffer, 1985; Clark, 1970; Davis, 1971; Goldstein, 1975, 1977).

Support for the paramilitary model. The thinking of the adherents of policing's paramilitary bureaucracy is not often found in the literature. It is to be found among the practitioners, most of whom argue that the nature of big-city police work—which often involves confronting violent criminals—requires a disciplined, occasionally military-like response, particularly when engaging armed and barricaded suspects (Bittner, 1970; Goldstein, 1975). The practitioners also contend that a paramilitary orientation helps to curb corruption and other potential police abuses and that it builds esprit de corps. This is the view also of Wilson and McLaren (1972), whose *Police Administration* has been studied for years by police officers seeking promotion within their departments.

Concepts of Organizational Culture

> For the manager the message is "Give culture its due."
> —Edgar H. Schein
> (1985:314)

Organizational culture, according to Block (1987), Schien (1985), Bradford and Cohen (1984), Peters and Waterman (1982), and many others, is an extraordinarily powerful phenomenon. It plays a role in and helps to explain organization successes and failures. It is easy, according to Schein, to confuse culture with other "useful concepts," such as climate, values, or corporate philosophy. Organizational culture "operates at one level below these others and largely *determines* them. Climate, values and philosophy can be managed in the traditional sense of management; but...it is not at all clear whether the underlying culture can be" (1985:314).

This section examines the definition of organizational culture, elements of organizational culture, organizational politics, police culture and community relations, and symbolic interactionism.

Culture Defined

Schein (1985:9) defined organizational culture as a

> pattern of basic assumptions—invented, discovered, or developed by a given group as it learns to cope with its problems of external adaptation and internal integration—that has worked well enough to be considered valid and, therefore, to be taught to new members as the correct way to perceive, think, and feel in relation to those problems.

The similarities between "culture" and "structure" are apparent. No effort will be made here to distinguish in detail between the two concepts. (The structural theorists argue that culture is a part of structure; the cultural theorists, for the most part, contend that structure is an element of culture.)

Schein, in acknowledging the pervasiveness of culture, raised and answered an important question (1985:48):

> Is there a danger that if culture is pervasive it is irrelevant? No more so than it is irrelevant for humans to understand how gravity and the atmosphere work. It is precisely the pervasiveness that makes it easy to ignore, however, in that it is hard to get a handle on something that is pervasive. But failing to understand how culture works is just as dangerous in the organizational world as failing to understand gravity...in the...physical world.

42

Elements of Organizational Culture

Figure 2-2 presents elements or "levels" of culture, as defined by Schein. The basic assumptions actually constitute the *essence* of culture in Schein's model. Values and behavior are "observed manifestations of the cultural essence" (1985:14).

Artifacts. Schein's first level of culture, furthest from the essence or the "basic assumptions" of culture, is "artifacts," which he identifies as the most conspicuous level. The observer can see and hear cultural patterns.

American law enforcement offers even the casual witness a rich repertoire of cultural artifacts and creations. Commercial television carries—and has for years—dramatic and comedy series with police as the theme; documentaries and newscasts of major events involving the police are common, as are films. Two early works of Joseph Wambaugh (1970, 1972), in particular, capture the visible and audible aspects of the police culture. However, as Schein points out, these artifacts may be visible but they are often undecipherable, particularly to those outside the culture.

It is not uncommon even for people within the same culture to misread or misunderstand the meaning of what is seen or heard within the culture (Srivastva et al., 1984:297):

> [O]rganizational experience indicates that
> what one hears is not what was said, what
> one sees is not what was presented, what
> one promised is not what was delivered,
> what one feels is not what is expressed, and
> what one thinks is not what has happened.

Values. The second level of culture, according to Schein, is values. "In a sense all cultural learning ultimately reflects someone's original values, their sense of what 'ought' to be, as distinct from what is" (1985:15). Schein argues that, when

43

Figure 2-2
Schein's Levels of Culture

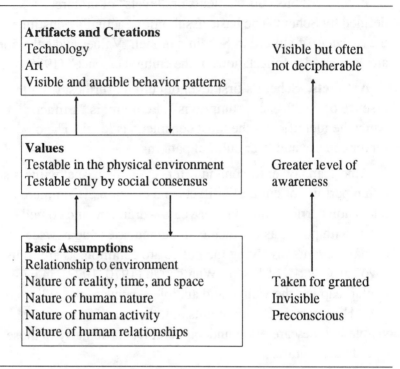

Source: Schein, 1985

Reprinted with permission from Schein, Edgar H. *Organizational Culture and Leadership: A Dynamic View*, Figure 1, page 14. Copyright 1985 by Jossey-Bass Inc., Publishers. For use by the Police Executive Research Forum, 1992. All rights reserved. May not be resold.

confronted with a new problem or challenge, someone in the organization, often the founder or the leader, will suggest a solution. If the solution is successful, the value "gradually starts a process of *cognitive transformation* into a belief and, ultimately, an assumption....[The value] drop[s] out of consciousness, just as habits become unconscious and automatic" (1985:16).

Value formation and value transformation take place, of course, at all levels in the law enforcement organization. What may be valued as desirable or good at one level of the hierarchy may be seen as deplorable at another. Many police administrators, for example, view "choir practice"[*] with horror, while many police officers view administrators' apparent loss of contact with the "real world" with equal disdain (Wambaugh, 1970, 1972).

Basic assumptions. Schein's "basic assumptions" correspond to Argyris' (Argyris and Schon, 1978) "theories-in-use," that is, they are firmly embedded in the way people in the organization think, feel, and act. As such, they are exceedingly difficult not only to change but even to confront. The field of law enforcement is replete with many such theories in use. Kelling and colleagues (1974) recount the difficulty encountered both in Kansas City and elsewhere in the police community during the preventive patrol experiment. Civilian review boards, now a reality in many American cities, were— and are—to most police administrators an anathema; there *is* no justification for them (Geller, 1985). Police unionism, to many administrators, is just as evil (Bouza, 1985).

How leaders and managers behave in a police department is, in large part, a function of the assumptions they make about themselves, their work, and the world around them—including other people. McGregor's (1960) classic "Theory X-Theory Y" typology, while perhaps limited from a strategic point of

---

[*]An after-hours social activity common among police officers that is characterized by heavy consumption of alcohol and loud, boisterous, often profane camaraderie, with an occasional accidental wounding of one of the participants. Given its name by Wambaugh (1970), it is not unlike the behavior of London's Metropolitan Police Department's Criminal Intelligence Division (CID) officers described by Van Maanen in "Power in the Bottle: Informal Interaction and Formal Authority" in Srivastva (1986).

view, maintains its currency as a theoretical construct. Many of the assumptions that create and maintain tension in support of the paramilitary bureaucracy, as well as the autocratic practices of some police chief executives, are founded in the belief that officers cannot be trusted (Berkley, 1969; Goldstein, 1975, 1977; Sherman, 1985). That the history of U.S. law enforcement (Fosdick, 1969; Smith, 1940; Vollmer, 1936) may support that view does little to illuminate contemporary practices and needs.

Organizational Politics

> There is no more engaging and volatile aspect of work life than the dimension of organizational politics. In most places, people are not comfortable discussing politics openly. Politics in organizations is like sex was in the 1950s—we knew it was going on, but nobody would really tell us about it. (Block, 1987:5)

Stages of work team development: Origins of organizational politics. Bradford and Cohen (1984) suggest that there are discernible stages to the development of a work team. Bearing resemblance to the theories of group dynamicists (Schein, 1969; Schutz, 1958; Shaw, 1981), Bradford and Cohen's stages of work team development also bring into focus significant aspects of organizational politics.

Five stages of development are identified: (1) *membership,* in which individuals struggle with issues of identity and inclusion; (2) *subgroup,* in which individuals begin to gravitate toward others who are like them; (3) *confrontation,* in which subgroup members, seeing other subgroups as "too naive, too political, too narrow, too philosophical—in short, 'not like us' " (Bradford and Cohen, 1984:191)—move from "polite subgrouping" to aggressive confrontation with the other group(s);

46

(4) *individual differentiation*, in which group members, no longer needing the permanent support of their subgroups, begin to act independently; and (5) *shared responsibility*, in which individuals, dedicated to the organization's "overarching goal," act in a mature, interdependent fashion with one another.

Bradford and Cohen observe that most work teams never achieve the sense of shared responsibility of stage five. Indeed, they believe that most chief executives would consider themselves fortunate to have an organization whose members act with the professional independence and maturity suggested in the individual differentiation of stage four. What keeps an organization from achieving shared responsibility for success? Already suggested in this chapter are structural and cultural explanations. Block (1987) provides a more specific answer: politics.

Organizational power. Block defines politics as "the pursuit of power." Power, he offers, "is both a function of position in the hierarchy and, more importantly, a state of mind" (1987:59). It is more, according to French and Raven's (1959) classic research. They identified five bases of social power, with French adding a sixth in 1970: (1) reward power, (2) coercive power, (3) legitimate power, (4) expert power, (5) referent power, and (6) informational power. Each base of power (as well as a seventh, "relationship" power, suggested by some theorists) can play a large role in organizational politics. But it is *expert* power and *referent* power that best suit Block's definition of the politics of "enlightened self-interest."

Nonmanipulative politics. Block (1987:xiv) observes that "Manipulation is so ingrained in our way of doing business that we often do not recognize it. Even if we are aware that we are engaged in a process of manipulation, we rationalize it by

47

saying that it is a fact of life and it is the only way to get things done." As an alternative, he offers under the heading "Developing Antidotes for Bureaucracy" elements of enlightened self-interest that, he contends, can change the meaning of organizational politics (1987:80–86):

- *Enlightened Self-Interest No. 1: Meaning.* Block is suggesting here that individuals commit themselves to work that is "genuinely needed" and that expresses their values.

- *Enlightened Self-Interest No. 2: Contribution and Service.* This calls for individuals to treat the organization as if it belongs to them and to view and treat other organizational units as if they were customers.

- *Enlightened Self-Interest No. 3: Integrity.* The call here is to tell the truth to all people at all times.

- *Enlightened Self-Interest No. 4: Positive Impact on Others' Lives.* Block argues that individuals, when in the organizational setting, tend to suspend strong personal or religious beliefs and values about how other people should be treated. They can act in their own self-interest by caring deeply about the well-being of their colleagues.

- *Enlightened Self-Interest No. 5: Mastery.* This final self-interest reflects a pride and self-satisfaction that comes from the individual knowing, understanding, and performing his or her work better than anyone else. It places emphasis on learning.

Power sharing. The realization of Block's new definition of organizational politics suggests the value, if not the necessity, of sharing power within the organization (Bennis and Nanus, 1985; Bradford and Cohen, 1984; Hickman and Silva, 1984; Tjosvold, 1984; Townsend, 1984). Nowhere is this likely to have a more immediate and significant effect than at the top of the organization.

Bass (1981:170) offers a plausible, but untested, hypothesis that the followers of powerful leaders are likely to be more powerful than the followers of less powerful leaders. While there appears to be no empirical evidence to support this, Abdel-Halim (1983) did find that when "power equalization" among employees is achieved, and when it is experienced at all levels, it helps top managers better understand and respond to changes in the relative distribution of power. That, he concluded, enhances the manager's effectiveness in managing the organization.

The Police Culture and Community Relations

This section draws upon the literature to form a more focused discussion by developing the relationship between police culture and police-community relations. The ideas expressed below are influenced by Schein's (1985:3) admonition that "[u]nless we learn to analyze...organizational cultures accurately, we cannot really understand why organizations do some of the things they do and why leaders have some of the difficulties that they have."

The police officer's "working personality." Skolnick (1966) pointed to danger and authority as two elements in the work of police officers that combine to form a *working personality*. He (1966:62) was troubled by the combination

> ...*danger* and *authority* found in the task of the policeman unavoidably combine to

frustrate procedural regularity. If it were
possible to structure social roles with
specific qualities, it would be wise to
propose that these two should never, for the
sake of the rule of law, be permitted to
coexist.

Danger, argues Skolnick, so easily arouses fear and anxiety
that it can cause individuals to behave in irrational ways, to do
things under its influence they would not otherwise do.[*]
Authority, on the other hand, requires calm and reflective judgment for its wise exercise. It is where danger and authority in-
tersect that Skolnick believes policing faces its greatest test.

Police-community partnership. In a chapter entitled "The
Symbolic Assailant and Police Culture," Skolnick (1966:45)
states,

> The *raison d'etre* of the policeman and the
> criminal law, the underlying collectively
> held moral sentiments which justify penal
> sanctions, arises ultimately and most clear-
> ly from the threat of violence and the
> possibility of danger to the community.

This suggests the need for the police officer to be a part of,
rather than apart from, the community. Much has been written
in support of police-community partnerships as a means to
(1) better relations with the community (Brown, 1985; Kelling,
1985; Reiss, 1985; Rumbaut and Stamper, 1974; Williams,

---

*In a training program for San Diego police officers (Task Force on
Human Relations Training, 1986), George Thompson presented principles of *Verbal Judo* (Thompson and Stroud, 1984). Thompson suggests that officers need to understand that most of the people they encountered are "under the influence," if not of alcohol or other drugs then
of anger or despair or confusion or pain. Rarely, owing to the circumstances that bring them into contact with the police or because of the
impact of the officer's authority, do people behave "normally" in the
presence of a uniformed cop.

1985); (2) more effective crime fighting (Stamper et al., 1981; Sweeney and Ellingsworth, 1973); and (3) officer safety (Adams et al., 1985; Officer Safety Task Force, 1985). But there is little evidence of *long-term* successful efforts in improving police-community relations (Punch, 1985; Sherman, 1985; S. Walker, 1985).

Social isolation and police solidarity. Skolnick takes his theory of the influence of danger and authority in shaping a police officer's "working personality" a step further and helps to explain how the *culture* of policing functions as a barrier to improved relations with the community. He writes of two inevitable outcomes of the working personality: (1) social isolation and (2) police solidarity. Those two phenomena help to explain why American police are imbued with a "we-they" predisposition in their thinking and behavior, according to Skolnick.

There are other factors, as well, that contribute to social isolation and police solidarity: the *work schedule* of police officers that causes them to miss holidays and other important family events, to work nights and attend school and court during the day, and to experience psychological and physiological maladjustment in attempting to cope with their hours (Droge, 1973; Reiss, 1971); the pressure on *intimate relationships* (T. Walker, 1969; Wambaugh, 1970); the *confusion* and *cynicism* that come from conflicting expectations of their bosses, the courts, and the public (Niederhoffer, 1969; Rubinstein, 1973); and the feeling of *powerlessness* in attempting to counter what they view as an unfair characterization of police officers in the media (Skolnick and McCoy, 1985).

Toch, Grant, and Galvin (1975) see the behavioral consequences of these culture-shaping influences as extraordinarily complex and multidimensional, making it all but impossible for an "outsider" to understand. Consequently, that places more distance between the officer and the community, even as it fortifies police solidarity.

Symbolic Interactionism

Quite apart from what determines or influences culture, the mechanism by which it is formed and translated is *symbolic interaction*. Lauer and Handel (1983:87) defined symbols as

> ...learned, shared meanings that distinguish human behavior. Symbols enable us to transcend the immediate situation, the present. And symbol systems are the basis for social order, for our understanding of reality, for our cognitive processes, and for our overt behavior.

"Interaction," according to Lauer and Handel, is the "reciprocally influenced behavior of two or more people. That is, when two people interact, each influences the behavior of the other and each directs one's own behavior on the basis of the other's behavior towards one" (1983:87).

The value of symbolic interactionism in understanding culture cannot be overestimated, nor can the practical implications for leaders. As Lauer and Handel make clear, *shared* symbols lead to cohesiveness. If great social distance exists between police and community (Brown, 1985) or between police officers and their leaders (Reuss-Ianni, 1983), significant progress in police reform is unlikely. This conclusion is supported by the work of researchers Dean and Brass (1985), who found that increased social interaction leads to a convergence of perceptions. That is, people who spend time together tend to view the world in similar ways.

Cialdini (1985) wrote, "Especially in an ambiguous situation, the tendency for everyone to be looking to see what everyone else is doing can lead to a fascinating phenomenon

52

called 'pluralistic ignorance' " (1985:110). It is reasonable to assume that, in such situations, the opportunity for leadership may be great, particularly if the leader and the group share the same symbols and if the social distance between leader and group is not great.

Such opportunities, "ambiguous situations," are common in law enforcement; they present a special challenge to the police chief, given that "the human is a cognitive creature who functions in a context of shared meanings which are communicated through language" (Lauer and Handel, 1983:82). Many of these ambiguous situations stem from an incident in the community that requires not merely an explanation but an expression of meaning, as well. Schein (1985) calls such incidents, and other significant happenings in the life of an organization, "catalytic marker events." Those marker events may affect profoundly the chief executive's attitude and future behavior toward the organization's employees, the community, the media, and others. They may affect in similar fashion the attitudes and behavior of the officers toward the community and the chief.

Functions and Processes of Leadership

Examined to this point has been the literature of the field of law enforcement as well as that of organizational structure and culture. Attention is now turned to the place of leadership in the organization. This section reviews the literature on leadership theories, the leadership function (vision and greatness), and leader behavior.

Leadership Theories

Luthans (1985:479–480) summarizes six theories of organizational leadership, each explaining, from a different point of view, how leaders emerge to exert power and influence:

(1) leaders are born, not made—the "Great Man" theory of leadership; (2) individuals exhibit certain characteristics or traits that are valued by followers and are, therefore, accorded leadership status; (3) leaders are supported by the composition and dynamics of the group; (4) certain people emerge as leaders as a product of the *zeitgeist* (German for "spirit of the times"); (5) individuals follow a "path-goal" process, becoming leaders by design; and (6) leadership may be seen as a synthesized combination of all or most of these theories, a view taken by the behaviorally oriented social learning theorists.

Most writers appear to support the idea that the six theories have evolved, reflecting increased sophistication and increasingly greater validity, much in the order of their presentation here, with the "social learning" theory the most useful.

The Leadership Function: Vision and Greatness

Burns (1978:1) argues that the world is experiencing a "crisis of leadership." He attributes this crisis to the "mediocrity or irresponsibility of so many of the men and women in power." Arguing that "leadership rarely rises to the full need for it," Burns maintains that "[t]he fundamental crisis underlying mediocrity is intellectual...we know far too little about *leadership*." He (1978:19) offers this definition of leadership:

> I define leadership as leaders inducing followers to act for certain goals that represent the values and the motivations—the wants and needs, the aspirations and expectations—*of both leaders and followers.* And the genius of leadership lies in the manner in which leaders see and act on their own and their followers' values and motivations.

Followers as leaders. This focus on the needs and wants of others, of *followers*, has taken the leadership literature far beyond its preoccupation with management "style," attitudes about "human nature," and desirable levels of "employee participation." It is taking seriously the heretofore radical notion that the role of leaders is to serve the people working for them. Greenleaf (1973), for example, saw the essence of leadership in the character of Leo in *Journey to the East* by Herman Hesse. Leo is by nature a servant, which is the key to his greatness. The "leadership myth," contend Kouzes and Posner (1987:xvi), "portrays the leader as a renegade who magnetizes a band of followers with courageous acts. In fact, leaders attract followers not because of their willful defiance but because of their deep respect for the aspirations of others."

Although a work on political leadership, Burns's 1978 book has inspired a major shift in the thinking of organizational theorists. Common are contemporary works that explicate Burns's belief that the function of the leader is to transform followers into leaders and leaders into moral agents (Block, 1987; Bradford and Cohen, 1984; Kouzes and Posner, 1987).

Visions of the future. Articulating—and "living"—a vision for the future that encompasses a deep concern for others in the organization as well as for one's customers or clientele is the focus of such writers as Bass (1985); Bennis and Nanus (1985); Block (1987); Kauffman (1980); Kiefer and Senge (1984); Kiefer and Stroh (1984); Kouzes and Posner (1987); Luthans (1985); Naisbitt (1982); and Peters and Waterman (1982).

This focus on the future is not new. Cornish (1977) quotes Jean Paul Sartre from one of the great existentialist's lectures in 1946: "You are free. Choose, that is to say, invent." Sartre, however, went on to say that "[n]o general system of ethics can tell you what to do." Stern (1967:85) quotes Boris, a figure from Sartre's novels, "The individual's duty is to do what he wants to do, to think whatever he likes, to be accountable to no one but himself, to challenge, again and again, every idea and every person."

Spiritual leadership. Today's organization and leadership theorists, including especially those listed above, seem to support strongly the notion that individuals can "invent the future." But they reject, just as strongly, the idea that one is "accountable to no one but himself" (Stern, 1967:85). Indeed, there is a distinctive thread of morality and spirituality that emerges from their discussion of leader responsibility to other people. McKnight (1984) makes it explicit in an article entitled "Spirituality in the Workplace." Ritscher (1986:61) defines "spiritual leadership" as a sense of vitality or esprit de corps that "draws on a spiritual force and hence cuts through to a deeper level and is more effective in creating a vital and effective [organization]."

Kouzes and Posner (1987:110–111) cite Martin Luther King, Jr.'s "I have a dream" speech of August 28, 1963, as an outstanding example of visionary leadership. It eloquently articulates fundamental values of the "American dream" and envisions a new future "transformed into a situation where little black boys and black girls will be able to join hands with little white boys and white girls and walk together as sisters and brothers."

This trend toward a more deeply purposeful form of leadership, to an inspired vision of the future, and to seeing greatness in oneself and in others may be a response to economic pressures or to slipping confidence in American organizational leadership. Mitchell and Scott (1987), citing a Gallup Poll, report that public confidence in American institutions has remained relatively stable over the past 13 years. Confidence in *leaders,* on the other hand, has declined precipitously.

56

Sherman (1985:462) reflects on police leadership in the country: "What many police executives appear to have done is to replace 'prosperity' with 'survival.' If prosperity means increasing success at accomplishing organizational goals, few police executives have achieved it. Nor have they decided to try."

Ouchi's (1981) book contains an appendix with statements of several American companies' corporate objectives, philosophies, values, and the like. A common thread is those organizations' quest for excellence—and for profit, to be sure. But there is also an unmistakable commitment to honesty, integrity, fairness, and concern for others. Regardless of motive, it appears certain that many American corporations are adopting organizational values not customarily associated with "business."

The benefits of those new organizational values, according to Kouzes and Posner's research (1987), are found in significantly higher levels of job satisfaction, commitment, loyalty, esprit de corps, clarity about the organization's values, pride in the organization, organizational productivity, and encouragement to be productive.

Characteristics of vision. In defining vision as *"an ideal and unique image of the future,"* Kouzes and Posner (1987:85) use four characteristics to describe the vision of a leader or of an organization: (1) it is something that can be "seen," that is, it evokes images and pictures; (2) it reflects a future orientation; (3) it suggests an ideal, a standard of excellence; and (4) it is unique to the leader or the organization. They go on to suggest that "[t]o create visions, leaders must become preoccupied with the future. They must be able to project themselves ahead in time" (1987:88).

This capacity to "see" into the future is described by former professional football coach Vince Lombardi:

The best coaches know what the end result
looks like, whether it's an offensive play, a
defensive play, a defensive coverage, or
just some area of the organization. If you
don't know what the end result is supposed
to look like, you can't get there. All the
teams basically do the same things. We all
have drafts, we all have training camps, we
all have practices. But the bad coaches
don't know what the hell they want. The
good coaches do.

Cited in Kouzes and Posner (1987:89), Lombardi's statement
was made to John Madden in response to a question about differences between good coaches and bad coaches. Kouzes and
Posner maintain that "[w]hat holds true for good coaches also
holds true for good leaders."

Leader Behavior

Now hear this
Now hear this

This is the captain speaking
This is the captain speaking

That is all
That is all

That "old navy proverb," cited in Block (1987:46), wryly
captures the attitude prevalent in early police administration
literature (Fosdick, 1969; Smith, 1940; Vollmer, 1936). The
police chief was urged to develop and exhibit *command
presence,* to be perceived as a "leader" at all costs—even if
there was no message to communicate, no destination toward
which to lead people. Even today, Iannone (1987) attaches

great importance to the need to cultivate "command presence," and Skousen (1977) suggests that chiefs "look busy" so they will not get interrupted. Presumably losing currency as police chief executives turn increasingly to professional and academic literature of greater consequence (Geller, 1985; Scott, 1986), this emphasis on form over substance does little to inspire either the community or the organization's employees.

Structured expectations. Bass (1981:200) cites evidence that the "most desired behavior of the leader is to structure expectations." Viewed broadly, this may be taken to mean the creation and articulation of a personal vision (Block, 1987; Burns, 1978; Kiefer and Senge, 1984; Kiefer and Stroh, 1984) or the development of an organizational mission statement, goals, and objectives (Drucker, 1973; Wilson and McLaren, 1972). It may also be taken to mean that a critical leader behavior is that of setting and enforcing standards of personal performance and conduct (Hersey, 1984; Iannone, 1987; Stamper, 1977). In short, desirable leadership behavior includes (1) standing for something; (2) charting an organizational course; and (3) communicating expectations and monitoring performance, such that those expectations become "structured."

Honesty. From Burns (1978) to Block (1987), the literature that pays particular attention to the spiritual dimension of leadership, whether of a sacred-religious or a secular-humanistic orientation, attaches great significance to honesty. Fisher and Ury (1981) offer an alternative to the process of negotiation—a crucial leadership function in law enforcement and elsewhere—that is based fundamentally on "telling the truth." Kouzes and Posner (1987) report that honesty was selected more frequently than any other quality in the studies they conducted. Block (1987:90) suggests that

> Our role models should be six-year-olds.
> They talk straight. They agree, they

disagree, they like, they hate, they say yes, they say no. Period. After age six, our education, life experience, and general sophistication teach us to be cautious about communicating our real intent. If we feel that we cannot say no, then our yes's don't mean anything.

"Honest in thought and deed" begins a line of the Law Enforcement Code of Ethics (Bristow, 1975). Much of the work in developing standards for law enforcement reflects a major concern about honesty and integrity in policing (American Bar Association, 1973; Bristow, 1975; President's Commission on Law Enforcement and Administration of Justice, 1967; *The Knapp Commission Report on Police Corruption*, 1973; National Advisory Commission on Criminal Justice Standards and Goals, 1973; National Commission on Law Observance and Enforcement, 1968; U.S. Congress House Subcommittee on Criminal Justice, 1984; S. Walker, 1985).

A commitment to truth—the facts as one sees them—is valued throughout the literature. The central theme is that the leader, in structuring expectations, would do well to set an explicit standard and serve as an example of honesty, integrity, and ethical behavior.

Self-awareness, awareness of others. It is "only in recognizing their own fallibility," writes Srivastva (1984:298),

> that executives are able to avoid making decisions or taking actions that are unrealistic rather than idealistic. There is a clarion call here for greater self-awareness, particularly during periods of success, when theories-in-use may go unquestioned until some irrevocable catastrophe makes them obviously untenable.

Bennis was asked in an interview by Ghiselin (1987b) whether he saw the leaders he had studied (Bennis and Nanus, 1985) as "constantly open to feedback." The answer was "Yes. When it had to do with the work, the job, the company, they were wide awake. They were the greatest askers, the greatest listeners I've ever met. You know that phrase, 'Feedback is the breakfast of champions'? Like that" (Ghiselin, 1987b:3).

Intuition. Leader *intuition*, and leader awareness of its potency and use in organizational decision making, appears to be gaining legitimacy in the literature (Block, 1987; Kiefer and Senge, 1984; Kiefer and Stroh, 1984; Kouzes and Posner, 1987). Gardner (Ghiselin, 1986:8) maintains that a "first class leader is communicating only partly in words. And the conversation between first class leaders and devoted followers is a good deal unconscious. It's intuitive. It's there." (Moreover, Gardner goes on to say, "...it's a shame to educate young people away from an understanding of that.")

A large intuitive capacity "depends upon an ability to get along with people—to be...empathetic and objective," according to Portnoy (1986:160). These qualities are necessary, he argues, because "people are dynamic, that is, their behaviors change at hair-raising speeds....The leader who understands the utility of...neurological programming can often restore rational behavior by reducing...anxiety" (1986:160). Whether the leader is trained in neurological or neurolinguistic programming, the case is made that he or she must have a solid understanding of why people behave the way they do in the organizational setting (Argyris and Schon, 1978; Cartwright and Zander, 1968; Schein, 1985; Shaw, 1981).

Kouzes and Posner (1987:93) suggest that

> Intuition is the wellspring of vision. In
> fact, by definition, intuition and vision are

directly connected. Intuition has as its root
the Latin word meaning "to look at." Intuition, like vision, is a "see" word. It has to
do with our abilities to picture and to
imagine.

The leader as "living emblem." In the film, *A Passion for Excellence,* Peters (1984) characterizes the effective leader as the "living emblem" of his or her organization, by which he means that the leader embodies the principles and beliefs of the organization. As the personification of what the organization stands for and believes in, the powerful leader is visible and conspicuous. His or her presence is felt by the customers or the clientele and by members of the organization.

Hunsaker and Alessandra (1980) argue that the leader must, to this end, have excellent interactive and overall communication skills, questioning effectively, listening actively, using body language to his or her best advantage. They also maintain that leaders must be constantly mindful of "spatial relations." Their hairstyle, clothing, indeed their "personal colors," need to be in tune with the leadership image they are expected to project.

While image is clearly an important dimension of executive leadership, Goldstein (1977:231), addressing himself to the nation's police chiefs, cautions,

> Few things are quite so inimical to improve-
> ment in the police field as the personable,
> attractive, articulate, and perhaps colorful
> police official whose strongest qualifica-
> tion for heading a police agency consists in
> his ability to fend off all attacks made
> upon it.

To increase the likelihood of a more effective and inspired leadership, Srivastva (1984:299) suggests that what is needed is "executive thinking...[that is] mindful, active, consequential and farsighted....[The] executive's supreme success is experienced not when leading but when being carried along by others toward the dream he or she wishes to fulfill."

Leader traits. Bass (1981) reports that, although the *situation* influences the type and quality of organizational leadership, there is strong evidence that certain personal traits are valuable, if not essential, to the leader. Hundreds of specific traits were analyzed, ranging from physical characteristics to intelligence, with Bass (1981:81) concluding,

> The leader is characterized by a strong drive for responsibility and task completion, vigor and persistence in pursuit of goals, venturesomeness and originality in problem solving, drive to exercise initiative in social situations, self-confidence and sense of personal identity, willingness to accept consequences of decision and action, readiness to absorb interpersonal stress, willingness to tolerate frustration and delay, ability to influence other persons' behavior, and capacity to structure social interaction systems to the purpose at hand.

Kouzes and Posner emphasize Bass's "readiness to absorb interpersonal stress" in arguing that "people cannot lead if they are not psychologically hardy. People will not follow others who avoid stressful events and who will not take decisive action" (1987:68). Kouzes and Posner also suggest that leaders must work to create an organizational atmosphere that encourages psychological hardiness in others.

Summary of traits and characteristics. In surveys of over 2,600 U.S. managers, Kouzes and Posner (1987) found strong support for the traits identified by Bass and others. The researchers asked that the managers list traits needed in an effective manager or leader. Their results are listed in *Table 2-1.*

The Executive's Role in the Managerial Process

> If *run* means to set policies, priorities, and mechanisms to ensure both achievement and accountability, there are major voids. That is, *no one* runs the police. (Mayo, 1985:411)

What does it mean, precisely, to *run* a police organization, or any organization? What differences, if any, exist between the functions of leadership and management? Emerging in the literature and, to an increasing degree, in organizational practice are some very clear answers to these questions (Kouzes and Posner, 1987; Ouchi, 1981). One thing seems obvious: there *is* a difference between leading and managing, and the difference is important. This section examines the manager's role versus the leader's role, management versus manipulation, and the police leader's managerial challenge.

The Manager's Role Versus the Leader's Role

Empirical research on the distinction between leadership and management is lacking. Even *Stogdill's Handbook of Leadership* (Bass, 1981:7–15) offers no help. It does present several ways of viewing leadership, namely, as a focus of group processes, personality and its effects, the art of inducing compliance, the exercise of influence, an act or behavior, a form of persuasion, a power relation, an instrument of goal achievement, an emerging effect of interaction, a differentiated role, and the initiation of structure. It also contains a section with the promising heading "Leadership as a Differentiated Role," but, while it provides several definitions of effective leadership, it does not differentiate that function from management.

Table 2-1

Leadership Traits Identified in Kouzes and Posner's Surveys of U.S. Managers (N=2,615)

Characteristic	Ranking	Percentage of managers selecting
Honest	1	83
Competent	2	67
Forward-looking	3	62
Inspiring	4	58
Intelligent	5	43
Fair-minded	6	40
Broad-minded	7	37
Straightforward	8	34
Imaginative	9	34
Dependable	10	33
Supportive	11	32
Courageous	12	27
Caring	13	26
Cooperative	14	25
Mature	15	23
Ambitious	16	21
Determined	17	20
Self-controlled	18	13
Loyal	19	11
Independent	20	10

Source: Kouzes and Posner, 1987

Definitions. In much of the literature the terms *leader* and *manager* and *leadership* and *management* tend to be used synonymously. For this reason alone, Bass (1981:15) suggests that "[u]ntil an 'academy of leadership' establishes a standard definition, we must continue to live with both broad and narrow definitions, making sure to understand which kind is being used in any particular analysis." Hersey (1984:16) defines leadership as "any attempt to influence the behavior of another individual or group," and management as "working with and through others to accomplish organizational goals." Munro (1974) tends to draw the line between staff functions and political functions. While not made explicit by Burns (1978), it is possible, according to Kouzes and Posner (1987) to conceive of Burns's *transformational* leadership as a distinctively leadership phenomenon and his *transactional* leadership as belonging to the category of management. Bass (1985) takes a similar view. This approach is also consistent with Zaleznik's (1983) notion that leaders are inspired and guided by visions of the future, while managers are involved with the management of things past and present. In other words, leaders transform or create new states, while managers transact exchanges of existing conditions.

Kouzes and Posner (1987:27) contend that

> If there is a clear distinction between the process of managing and the process of leading, it is in the distinction between getting others to do and getting others to want to do. Managers, we believe, get other people to do, but leaders get other people to want to do.

Using the metaphor of leadership as a journey, much as Lerner (1987) uses it to describe life in general, Kouzes and Posner state that the origin of the root word *lead* is "to go."

Leaders, they contend, are those who "go first. They are those who step out to show others the direction in which to head. They begin the quest for a new order" (1987:32–33). Management, on the other hand, "seems to connote 'handling' things....A major difference between management and leadership can be found in the root meanings of the two words, the difference between what it means to handle things and...to go places." Zenger (1985) refers to leadership as management's "better half."

Williamson (1984:75), citing Bennis's "deceptively simple but insightful" distinction between leaders as "people who do the right thing" and managers as "people who do things right," argues that American business has come to be "dangerously overmanaged and underled...."

Antipathy toward management. This theme is common in the literature (Bradford and Cohen, 1984; Hickman and Silva, 1984; Peters and Waterman, 1982). Peters offers an especially harsh indictment of "management," calling it "one of the words I have most come to despise in the English language" (1984 film, *A Passion for Excellence*). His antipathy toward management is based on his perception that it is used by executives to tell, to order, to control, and, ultimately, to stifle their employees' imagination and to crush their spirit. Joined by Waterman (1982:29), Peters contends that

> The numerative, rationalist approach to management dominates the business schools. It teaches us that well-trained professional managers can manage anything. It seeks detached, analytical justification for all decisions. It is right enough to be dangerously wrong, and it has arguably led us seriously astray.

Kouzes and Posner (1987:xv) cite H. Ross Perot, in support of Peters and Waterman's concern about what is being taught in business schools: "People cannot be managed. Inventories can be managed, but people must be led." They also suggest that it is necessary for organizations to move away from the conventional managerial notion that "what gets rewarded is what gets done" to an orientation of "what is rewarding is what gets done."

The need for management and managers. But who gets the work done if the leader's role is to create a vision (Block, 1987), manage organizational culture (Schein, 1985), capture imaginations (Sorcher, 1985), function as the organization's "living emblem" (Peters, 1984), empower others (Srivastva et al., 1986), and "wander around," in the sense of "management by wandering around" (Peters and Waterman, 1982)?

Visionary leadership, it will be argued in the conclusion of this paper, is a full-time proposition for the police chief executive. But there are specific *managerial* tasks and duties that must be performed in the police department or in any organization (Drucker, 1973). "Doing things right" is essential. It is to the manager that the leader might look to ensure that the leader's standards of performance and conduct are set and enforced (Hsu and Marsh, 1983), and done so in a way that invites the meaningful participation of the work force (Jago, 1981); that progress toward goals and objectives is carefully monitored, reported, and controlled (Anderson and Reilly, 1981); that planning, coordination, and budgeting are carried out in a manner that adheres to the philosophy and the principles of the organization (Tjosvold, 1984).

Managers help leaders learn whether the organization is functioning, on the line, in the field, in the conference rooms, and in the offices the way their leaders have envisioned it functioning. Quality control requires time, attention, and clearly defined roles and responsibilities (Tetlock, 1985).

Managerial skills. Zaleznik (1983), as noted, argues that managers are guided by perspectives rooted in and determined by the traditions of the past. Leaders' perspectives are created by what they imagine (or "envision") the future to be. The skills of the manager, then, differ from those of the leader. Analytical, planning, budgeting, and coordinating skills are just a few of the qualities needed in a manager (Bass, 1981). However, Peters's protestations notwithstanding, it is difficult to conceive of an effective leader who is not also an effective manager. Indeed, the leader's very survival depends, in large measure, on his or her ability to master the managerial process (Barnard, 1968; Drucker, 1973). This is true especially if the leader delegates the management or the "running" of the organization to a manager. According to Bradford and Cohen (1984:2–3), "[e]ven the visions of supremely enlightened presidents must be translated into action by strong middle managers who can pull their subordinates together to achieve the increasingly difficult tasks necessary for organizational survival." Kouzes and Posner (1987) argue that both leadership and management are necessary to create and sustain healthy organizations.

The issue, therefore, may be framed as a question of how leaders spend their days or what kinds of activities occupy their time.

Time management. Schein (1985:2) argues that "[i]f the concept of leadership as distinguished from management and administration is to have any value, we must recognize the centrality of [the] culture management function in the leadership concept." The process of "embedding culture," it may be argued, is an extraordinarily time-consuming process, one that requires both patience and high energy. It requires the leader's undivided attention.

Yet, according to Mayo (1985), police chief executives spend their days in notoriously fragmented, unfocused ways. Mayo monitored the time utilization of three prominent police chiefs and found that they spend 50 percent of their total time at work on activities of less than 10 minutes duration. Only 5 percent is spent on activities of more than 60 minutes. In one week's time they handle 370 incoming and outgoing telephone calls and attend 17 scheduled meetings and 50 unscheduled meetings. Mayo contends that American police chiefs tend to move at a frenetic pace, often engaging in ill-conceived or poorly executed innovations, in part because of their awareness of the "markedly abbreviated" tenure of big-city chiefs; the average, as noted previously, is 2.8 years (Mayo, 1985).

Another reason might be that they are following the advice of writers like Skousen (1977:49):

> ...*Run a hot desk*. A chief who has a reputation for being extremely busy is less likely to be imposed upon by chronic complainants, gushing gossipers and casual callers who just happened to be passing by. A chief's office should have an atmosphere of "operating under pressure" since the rest of the department lights its fire from the work temperature which he creates. The chief should make the whole department conscious of the fact that "time is saved when time is used."

This advice to police chiefs is in marked contrast to the practices of an increasing number of executives of major corporations who are spending large amounts of time with employees on the shop floor and with customers or vendors in the field.

70

According to Kouzes and Posner (1987), at the time of their study Robert L. Swiggett, chairperson and chief executive officer of Kollmorgen Corporation, spends 25 percent of his time talking to company employees. Debi Coleman, factory manager of the Fremont facility of Apple Computer, spent five hours a day on the floor during the development of the Macintosh computer.

Mintzberg (1980) found that the average executive has nine minutes between interruptions. If, as Kouzes and Posner suggest, time spent on given activities is the "truest test of what the leader really thinks is important" (1987:202), the executive's ability to modify the structural arrangements of his or her work may be seen as an essential quality of "self-management."

Management Versus Manipulation

Block (1987:9) summarizes what he sees as a widespread tendency toward manipulation rather than management of the organization:

> Having grown up in a traditional hierarchical organization with patriarchal values, too many of us believe that in order to manage the politics of our situation, we must become good at: manipulating situations and, at times, people; managing information and plans carefully to our own advantage; invoking the names of high-level people when seeking support for our projects; becoming calculating in the way we manage relationships; paying great attention to what people above us want from us; living with the belief that in order to get ahead, we must be cautious in telling the truth.

These manipulative tendencies may be deeply embedded in the organization's culture (Schein, 1985). Indeed, as Block and others (Bradford and Cohen, 1984; Hickman and Silva, 1984) point out, the chief executive—while disturbed by such behavior—may have helped to create an organizational environment conducive to manipulative behavior. Often, the executive's very rise to the top is seen as the product of manipulation.

Value of nonmanipulative behavior. Recent research offers strong evidence of the value of nonmanipulative behavior in the organizational setting. Richmond, McCroskey, and Davis (1982) found that leader tolerance for disagreement between the boss and the worker leads to greater personal satisfaction of both parties. Participation and cooperation, according to Tjosvold (1984), are linked positively to strengthened work relationships, higher morale, improved productivity, and personal and organizational goal congruence. Tjosvold also found that leaders who demonstrate cooperation are perceived by their subordinates as making a contribution to the employees' job performance. The subordinates experience an increased desire to remain on the job, and they are more satisfied with their work. Finally, in support of increased autonomy and feelings of personal power, Kohn and Schooler (1982) found that self-directed work increases ideational flexibility and leads to a healthier orientation to one's self and to society.

Credibility. According to Kouzes and Posner (1987), it is critical that leaders and managers learn how they are perceived by their subordinates. If they lack credibility, for example, it is extremely difficult for them to be perceived as nonmanipulative. Credibility may be seen as the cumulative effect of the traits and characteristics listed in *Table 2-1*. Learning to use the term "we" rather than "I" offers, according to Kouzes and Posner, a simple, one-word test to learn whether one is likely to be perceived as a leader.

The Police Leader's Managerial Challenge

Mayo (1985:411), returning to the idea of "running" a police department, suggests that the term means to direct daily operations. With that definition in mind, he argues that "two things are clear: that police chiefs perform this function and that they should not." He contends that chiefs often resort to running, or managing, their own organizations because of incompetent or disloyal subordinates. (Or, perhaps because they are following Skousen's prescription and running a "hot desk.") Regardless of the reason, the effect, according to Mayo, is that, given the structural realities of their situation, chiefs are kept from providing leadership on "broad, long-term issues."

Ironically, the "busyness" of the police chief does not preclude a tendency toward isolation. McNamara (1985) contends that police chiefs are not kept, and do not seek to be kept, informed about certain kinds of information. He describes American police departments as "pressure boilers" with no warning or cutoff valves. Chiefs, he suggested, are preoccupied with minor details, inattentive to signs of organizational problems.

Hickman and Silva (1984:26) believe that "most top executives can either think strategically or build cultures creatively but cannot do both simultaneously. The challenge is to become both visionary and realistic, sensitive and demanding, innovative and practical." This statement embraces the idea that powerful leadership *and* effective management are requisites to effective policing in America.

The Effects of Organizational Structure and Culture on Executive Leadership and Management

Freeman (1986:5) captures a sense of the seemingly immutable patterns of the behavior of humans in bureaucracies in his review of Richard E. Neustadt and Ernest R. Mays' 1986 book, *Thinking in Time: The Uses of History for Decision Makers*:

> They know the usual course of decision making is not easily changed. Usual practice, we fear has six ingredients: a plunge toward action; over-dependence on fuzzy analogies, whether for advocacy, analysis or both; inattention to an issue's own past; failure to think a second time—sometimes even a first—about key presumptions; stereotyped suppositions about persons or organizations...and little or no effort to see choices as part of any historical sequence.

Freeman's review reinforces the significance of the cumulative effects of structure and culture on both executive leadership and executive management.

Effects of Bureaucracy

Eighteen years ago Toffler (1970) predicted the "death of bureaucracy" within 50 years. His prediction was based on the belief that the rigidity of the bureaucratic structure—its inability to respond to human needs and to accomplish organizational purposes—would cause those who lead bureaucracies to exchange them for "adhocracies."

Urging the decline of bureaucracy in policing. Increasing numbers of writers are attacking both the paramilitary and the bureaucratic nature of municipal law enforcement. Reiss (1985:62) argues that bureaucratically specializing responsibility for police-community relations, a response to widely publicized strains in the relationship during the 1960s and early 1970s, has been a "dismal failure." He argues further that other "fundamental transformations are required in organization, recruitment, training, and control of behavior in policing" if reform objectives are to be met.

Munro (1974:76–77) draws on a study of the Sears Roebuck Company to suggest that

> The elimination of many of the intervening ranks currently present in a police department would force superiors to delegate many responsibilities to their subordinates....The weight of empirical evidence would seem to indicate that in police organizations too much emphasis has been placed on the span of control principle as a relatively inflexible rule of management. The resulting many-layered command structure of the police department precludes effective decentralization of services, and too often, is dysfunctional from the point of view of attaining socially approved organizational goals.

Pressures for change. Finally, Roberg (1979:314) contends that there are "two prevailing conditions in police systems [that] necessitate, at least to some degree, the decline of highly bureaucratic structures and managerial styles." The first of those conditions is the growing realization that police departments must function within "turbulent environments." The second condition, writes Munro, is that law enforcement is attracting "young, highly educated, and demanding individuals," for whom, presumably, the rigid paramilitary bureaucracy is too confining.

More on Reason and Intuition

Fritz (1984) argues that many people have a "reactive-responsive" orientation, as opposed to a creative orientation. His view is that their feeling of powerlessness and their "closed system" way of looking at the world makes it very difficult for them to function effectively as leaders. Yet many of today's organizations suffer from structures and cultures that produce the reactive-responsive orientation. Rationality is valued, intuition and creativity devalued (Bradford and Cohen, 1984; Hickman and Silva, 1984; Peters and Waterman, 1982).

Pascale and Athos (1981) also saw that tendency in American business organizations, contrasting it with the Japanese suspicion of an excess of logic. "Rikutsupoi" is the Japanese word for "too logical," and the suggestion is that American business, suffering from this condition, has lost its economic advantage because of it.

The police hunch. In the police field, an irony emerges. If "intuition" may be seen as synonymous with "hunch," then the actual practices of police officers (T. Walker, 1969; Wambaugh, 1970, 1972; Whittemore, 1969) would lead to the conclusion that policing is a fertile breeding ground for intuition. A police officer's "sixth sense" is a common topic of discussion from police academy days on. Good police work, the arrest of a wanted suspect for example, is often the result of a hunch. Additionally, Whittemore (1969:11) writes that "[t]he cop's world allows him little time for working at reasonable conclusions." Successful police work requires quick thinking, imagination, intuition, and creativity.

Since the overwhelming majority of police chiefs have ascended through the ranks to become chief executives (Witham, 1985), it seems reasonable to assume that they would be blessed with exceptional intuitive powers, with a predisposition toward creativity. However, the literature neither confirms nor refutes this supposition. There is, on the other hand, ample evidence reflected throughout this chapter that police chief executives spend much of their time reacting to, rather than creating, situations.

Views of Human Nature

McGregor's (1960) Theory X-Theory Y typology, which contrasts two opposing points of view about the nature of human beings (from hard working and trustworthy, for example, to lazy and untrustworthy), needs to be placed in the context of structure (Kauffman, 1980) and culture (Schein, 1985). The contemporary literature makes no less relevant the basic premise of McGregor, but it does demand that leaders' assumptions about the motives of followers be analyzed in light of the powerful influences of structure and culture.

Link Between Police Practices and Leader Behavior: Implications for Change

There are indications throughout the literature of police administration, and the more general field of organizational leadership and management, that leader behavior both influences and is influenced by police practices on the streets. Numerous other variables function in the same way, that is, they act on the police chief and the chief acts on them. The behavior of individual chiefs and individual officers is the product of powerful interdependent, often conflicting expectations and influences. Most of these variables that affect behavior are rooted in political, structural, and cultural *systems* of enormous complexity (Kauffman, 1980). Police leaders inclined toward significant reform face formidable challenges, first in understanding their complicated world and, second, in changing it.

Addressed in this section are indications of change, risk, and commitment to a new future.

Indications of Change

Skolnick and Bayley (1986), using a "multi-ethnographic" research model, studied police departments in the cities of Santa Ana, Newark, Oakland, Denver, Houston, and Detroit. Those were agencies believed by the researchers to be strongly "community-oriented" and generally successful in their approach to policing. Skolnick and Bayley found four elements that, they suggest, are indications of a commitment to improved relations with the community and to police reform in general: (1) police-community reciprocity, (2) decentralization of command, (3) reorientation of patrol, and (4) increased civilianization of the department. The role of the leader in all this, they maintain, has been to "make it happen."

Police-community reciprocity. This element of the effort to improve relations with the community it serves is an indication of the chief executive's view that the community and the police are one, much in the spirit of Burns's idea that leaders and followers are one. Block (1987:119), in outlining his consulting firm's credo, captures the essence of the reciprocity element with "[w]e treat all people who come in contact with us as members of our organization."

Decentralization of command. The subject of continuing debate in police administration circles (Geller, 1985; Goldstein, 1975; Wilson and McLaren, 1972), the decentralization of police responsibility and authority was a feature of early American law enforcement in the larger cities (Fosdick, 1969; Smith, 1940). In the most common model, precincts or neighborhood stations were established, typically with a captain as the "commanding officer." The captain was given around-the-clock responsibility for policing his or her area.

78

While some functions (usually homicide, vice, narcotics, and intelligence) remained centralized and assigned to headquarters, the area station operated theoretically with substantial autonomy. The central rationale for such an arrangement was to put the police department in closer touch with the community it serves, fixing responsibility and authority for policing at the neighborhood level.

With the revelations of the Wickersham Commission in 1931 (National Commission on Law Observance and Enforcement, 1968), many agencies moved to recentralize command, on the supposition that greater control over corruption, brutality, and inefficiency would be realized. The centralization movement, coupled with significant other reforms, including the practice of rotating personnel from one beat or from one precinct to another, produced major improvements in American law enforcement (Skolnick and Gray, 1975). However, as the dialectic causes one to anticipate (Lauer, 1982), the centralization solution created its own set of problems, the most significant of which was the structural impossibility of true community-oriented policing. Consequently, the movement toward centralization was gradually reversed. Today, many agencies, bolstered by a belief that the problems that motivated the centralization trend have been ameliorated, are moving back toward the decentralized arrangement.

The San Diego Police Department offers an excellent example of the pattern of change. Formed in 1889, it decentralized by establishing several small "substations" as it grew. By midcentury, responding to evidence of inefficiency and corruption as well as concerns about communication and coordination, it returned to a highly centralized form of policing (although it did keep two substations, one in the northern part of the city, the other at the Mexican border). By the late 1970s, Chief Bill Kolender was convinced that the department needed to be decentralized in order to improve the agency's relationship with the community, its crime-fighting effectiveness, and its overall provision of police service. A massive, multimillion dollar decentralization project was undertaken, and today there are seven area stations—in addition to a new headquarters building—that serve a city of 400 square miles and over one million people.

Reorientation of patrol. The lessons learned in Kansas City (Kelling et al., 1974), San Diego (Boydstun, 1975; Boydstun et al., 1975; Rumbaut and Stamper, 1974), and in other cities that have experimented with traditional policing strategies have led to a major shift in thinking about uniformed police work. Many departments and communities are finding that "neighborhood watch," "fear reduction," and "problem-oriented policing" programs offer, as a supplement to preventive patrol, an effective alternative to random police patrolling (Geller, 1985). These programs encourage patrol officers to get out of their squad cars and interact with citizens in a variety of nontraditional ways. The results are mixed but generally favorable (Fyfe, 1985; Klockars, 1985; Skolnick and Bayley, 1986).

Increased civilianization. Skolnick and Bayley (1986) argue that police departments tend to use police officers in positions that could be filled by civilians. Such positions include those that do not require enforcement powers, areas such as budgeting, dispatching, records administration, crime analysis, and the like. "Civilianization," they contend, makes municipal policing less expensive and, by hiring individuals trained in their specialties and dedicated to careers in those fields, more effective. It may also, if nonsworn personnel are given leadership responsibilities as supervisors and managers, have a modest "demilitarizing" effect, breaking down barriers caused by rank or other paramilitary organizational conditions.

(The San Diego Police Department, in late 1987, hired a non-sworn director of human resources. His authority and ascribed status are fixed at the commander level, making him a part of the agency's management team. The purposes of this move are identical to those outlined in this section.)

In articulating principles similar in nature to Skolnick and Bayley's elements of improved police-community interaction, Brown (1985) argues that there are three conditions police departments must create: (1) collaboration with the community in planning, operations, and performance evaluation; (2) involvement of the entire police organization in efforts to improve relations with the community; and (3) a willingness of the police department to share its power with the community.

The theoretical orientation of these writers is supported by the research of Dean and Brass (1985), who found that through increased social interaction a convergence of perceptions is achieved. If police officers work more closely with the community, and if community members come to see themselves as a part of the police department, this enhanced social interaction should result in a tendency to see the work in similar terms. Similarly, if chief executives were to spend more time interacting with their field personnel, those who do the work and those who lead the work, according to Dean and Brass's findings, might come to a greater appreciation of each other's priorities.

An entrepreneurial approach. Some writers call for police chiefs to adopt a more political as well as a more entrepreneurial approach to their work. The chief, according to Hudnut (1985:27–28), needs to "expand his vision beyond the narrow confines of the internal workings of the police department," becoming more "politically responsive." Doig and Hargrove (1987) concluded on the basis of their biographical research into the lives of 13 government leaders that "entrepreneurial leadership" is possible even in the public setting. Drucker (1964:174), giving credit to French economist J. B. Say for coining the term "entrepreneur" in its original meaning in 1800, defines entrepreneurial leadership as the "deliberate commitment of present resources to an unknown and unknowable future."

Against the entrepreneurial approach. Kouzes and Posner (1987:38) suggest that, while "[l]eaders must be change agents and innovators," they "need not be entrepreneurs, if we mean by that term those who actually initiate and assume the risk for a new enterprise." They found in their research on the "personal best" efforts of their subjects that in fewer than half of the cases, was the work initiated by the subject. They reject, then, the idea that excellent leadership must necessarily be entrepreneurial or intrapreneurial. Indeed, in Burns's (1978) definition of transformational leadership, the impetus for the initiation of change might just as easily come from the followers as from the leader. Bradford and Cohen (1984) argue this line in their discussion of "leader as developer."

Risk

An authentic effort to change American law enforcement, or any other social institution, entails significant risk. Block (1987:104) contends that "[t]he dependent side of ourselves wishes to take a predictable path and to choose maintenance instead of greatness." This, he maintains, is the "bureaucratic choice." On the other hand, as Bass (1981, 1985) makes clear, most leaders see themselves as influential people, hence their concept of self-as-leader might be altered if confronted with Bass's labeling of the effort to change the behavior of others as *attempted* leadership.

The willingness to risk new behaviors is rooted in complex psychological phenomena (Argyris and Schon, 1978; Bass, 1981; Ghiselin, 1987a, 1987b; Lauer, 1982; Ross, 1987;

Wheelis, 1973), but it is also tied to commitment to a vision (Block, 1987; Kiefer and Senge, 1984; Kiefer and Stroh, 1984; Kouzes and Posner, 1987) and to one's "spirituality" (McKnight, 1984). Put differently, a belief, held strongly enough, will be sufficient to cause individuals to take risks even as dimensions of their own cognitive and affective psychological makeup work against taking such action (Cialdini, 1985).

Lauer (1982:185–186), arguing that "ideas—or, more particularly, ideologies—are independent variables in change," suggests that "...ideologies act by preventing, impeding, facilitating, or directing change." The deeply felt conceptualizations and the systemically grounded characteristics and dynamics of ideology, then, make clear the force behind ideologies in the effort to change—or to resist change—in American law enforcement.

Commitment to a New Future

Kiefer and Senge (1984:14) describe a point of view that is

> so pervasive it easily becomes an "absolute truth" and a "self-fulfilling prophesy": "Things don't work, and there's nothing I can really do about it. I'm dissatisfied, but I'm stuck in a system too big, too unresponsive, and too complex to influence.

This attitude, they write, "not only permeates most organizations and institutions, but is the root cause of our sense of powerlessness in tackling the problem of creating a sustainable society."

An alternative. Acknowledging the influence of McGregor (1960) and Forrester (1981), Kiefer and Senge (1984) and Kiefer and Stroh (1984) have adopted and advanced the concept of *metanoic* organizations in the development of a new organizational paradigm. "Metanoia," from the Greek, meaning "a fundamental shift of mind," was, according to Kiefer and Senge (1984:2), "used by early Christians to describe the reawakening of intuition and vision. Simply put, a metanoic organization operates with a conviction that it can shape its destiny."

Leaders who hold such a conviction, they argue, can have an extraordinarily powerful effect on their world, assuming they also embrace and work toward achieving five dimensions of metanoic organizations: (1) a deep sense of vision or purposefulness; (2) alignment around that vision, (3) empowerment of others, (4) structural integrity, and (5) the balance of reason and intuition. Kouzes and Posner (1987) posit five overlapping dimensions when they suggest that leaders should (1) challenge the process, (2) inspire a shared vision, (3) enable others to act, (4) model the way, and (5) encourage the heart.

Examples. Addressed in other sections of this chapter, those dimensions have been placed into practice in several U.S. corporations, according to case studies conducted by Kiefer and Senge (1984): Kollmorgen Corporation; Cray Research, Inc.; Analog Devices, Inc.; Dayton-Hudson, a 90,000-person retailing organization; Tandem Computer; Steak and Ale, a restaurant chain that is a division of Pillsbury; The Hanover Insurance Companies; W. L. Gore & Associates; and the Herman Miller Furniture Company. While American law enforcement has undergone significant change, as noted in the opening section of this chapter, there is no evidence of the kind of paradigmatic change described herein.

Effects of change. According to Kaplan (1986:1), when "organizations take a new direction, key jobs can change. New requirements and different criteria for effectiveness in high-level positions may have profound implications for the success of a new strategy." Argyris and Schon (1978:22) argue that new directions are often the result of significant conflict in an organization. They describe a process of "double-loop learning" that occurs when managers begin an analysis leading to the resolution of conflicting requirements. This results in conflict, restructuring of organizational norms, and "very likely a restructuring of strategies and assumptions associated with those norms which must then be imbedded in the images and maps which encode organizational theory-in-use."

Professionalization. In a strong call for the professionalization of American law enforcement, Clark (1970) argues for higher police salaries, more and better training, the development of an esoteric body of knowledge, and other conditions associated with the professions. His suggestions are motivated by a belief that the police are in the "middle" in American society, and that is where they should stay, avoiding shifts to the right or the left.

For too long, argue proponents of police reform (American Bar Association, 1973; Bittner, 1970; Chevigny, 1969; Geller, 1983, 1985; Goldstein, 1975, 1977; Murphy, 1985; Reiss, 1971, 1985; Rumbaut, 1977; Skolnick, 1966; and many others), the police have not kept faith with their constitutionally mandated commitment to neutrality. Nor, it is suggested by the bulk of the literature, have they been as effective and as responsive as they must be in order to develop and sustain public confidence in them. That, then, is the challenge for America's big-city police chiefs.

Chapter Three

ANSWERS TO RESEARCH QUESTIONS

This study sought answers to four major research questions:

1. What do America's big-city chiefs profess to value in relation to their community and organizational responsibilities?

2. Is there a distinction in the relative importance chiefs attach to executive leadership versus executive management functions or tasks?

3. Is the executive behavior of the police chiefs, as viewed by their immediate assistants, consistent with their professed values?

4. Are there differences in the professed values or the observed behavior of the police chiefs based on individual or contextual demographic variables?

Essential to an adequate understanding of the study's answers to those questions is a general familiarity with the research methodology. Thus, highlights of the methodology are presented first, followed by a question-by-question discussion of findings and conclusions.

Research Methodology Highlights

Figure 3-1 summarizes the highlights of the research methodology leading to the development of the police practices leadership survey, its distribution, and its analysis. The paragraphs below track the sequence of steps outlined by *Figure 3-1.*

To describe police agency chief executive officers in terms of their leadership-management orientations, a five-category leader-manager typology was developed. That typology can be viewed as a continuum, with "leader" at one extreme and "manager" at the other. Initially, the in-between categories were "leader-manager," "centrist," and "manager-leader." Those categories may be described as follows (see Glossary for full definitions):

1. Leader. At the polar extreme from that of the pure manager, the pure leader does little or no hands-on or detailed work and is oriented toward the future. The leader generates a common and inspiring vision for the organization.

2. Leader-manager. Though oriented toward the future, the leader-manager is more active than the leader in setting, monitoring, and controlling organizational objectives, priorities, and expectations for performance and conduct.

Figure 3-1
Research Methodology Highlights

A five-category leader-manager typology continuum was developed: leader, leader-manager, centrist, manager-leader, manager.

200 police leader and manager behaviors/functions (variables) were identified.

The 200 behaviors/functions were reduced to 125, which were field tested and then further reduced to 100, to be included in two sets of survey instruments (questionnaires), one sent to chiefs and the other to their assistants (the police leadership practices survey [PLPS]).

Figure 3-1 (continued)

An external panel of subject-matter experts reviewed the PLPS, as did research methodologists. As a result, certain leader-manager behaviors/functions were modified or replaced; the centrist category was deleted from the leader-manager continuum; the 100 leader-manager behaviors/functions were matched to, and equally divided among, the remaining four categories in the continuum. The behaviors/functions were expressed as statements, about which respondents' answers will be captured across a scale ranging from "5" (strongly agree) to "1" (strongly disagree).

PLPS passed a review by a two-person police panel.

PLPS was mailed to police agencies in cities of at least 200,000 population (except San Diego). Recipients were 72 chiefs and 144 of their assistants. Responses were received from 52 chiefs and 92 assistants.

Respondents' data were subjected to a variety of analyses. One of them justified (1) elimination of 35 of the 100 behaviors/functions (variables) listed on the PLPS and (2) assignment of the remaining 65 variables to either the leader (34 variables) or manager (31 variables) category. Substantive findings and answers to the research questions flowed from examining the "Leader-34" and "Manager-31" groupings of variables.

---

3. Centrist. This person occupies the precise middle ground between the pure leader and the pure manager.

4. Manager-leader. Oriented toward pure manager functions, the manager-leader gets out and about in the organization, has relatively little contact with the community, and is more interested in the organization's current image and reputation than in its place in the future.

5. Manager. At the polar extreme from that of the pure leader, the pure manager is seen as one who controls the

agency's resources and whose time is spent almost exclusively in the office, which serves as the "command center" for the organization and from which the lion's share of the agency's paper work originates.

Following the creation of the five-category leader-manager continuum, the researcher developed 200 descriptions of leader- and manager-related behaviors and functions. After a subjective review, those descriptions were reduced to 125. They were further reduced to 100 following a field test.

Subsequently, research methodologists and a panel of subject-matter experts recommended clarification, modification, or replacement of 16 of the 100 leader-manager behaviors or functions. Also recommended and implemented was elimination of the "centrist" category from what had been a five-category leader-manager continuum. Each of the remaining four categories was assigned, as appropriate, 25 descriptions of leader-manager behaviors or functions. Potential respondents, of course, were not informed about the leader-manager continuum, much less that the 100 descriptions had been allocated, in equal numbers, among the four categories in the continuum.

Those 100 descriptions were in the form of statements with which potential respondents—police chiefs and their immediate assistants—would be asked to indicate the extent of their agreement or disagreement. Maximum agreement would be indicated by the respondents' circling the number "5" opposite the statement, while maximum disagreement would be indicated by circling "1." Intermediate answers would be noted by respondents' circling one of the three alternative numbers—4, 3, or 2, depending on the strength of agreement or disagreement with the adjacent statement (see Appendix B).

After successfully passing a review by a two-person police expert panel, two survey instruments (questionnaires)—collectively referred to as the police leadership practices survey (PLPS)—were mailed to two sets of potential respondents:

(1) the police chief executive officers in each U.S. city of at least 200,000 in population (except San Diego) and (2) two of each chief's immediate assistants. Given those criteria, 72 chiefs and 144 assistants received the PLPS.

As noted in Appendix B, chiefs were asked whether they believed that they should do what the 100 leader-manager descriptions or statements indicated. Assistants were asked whether they perceived that their chiefs actually did what the 100 leader-manager statements described. Chiefs and assistants were also both asked about such personal characteristics as age, sex, race, and time served in law enforcement and in their present agencies. Fifty-two chiefs and 92 assistants (67 percent response rate) replied. They represented 28 states and 76 percent of the 72 cities targeted by the survey.

Determined by the number circled (1, 2, 3, 4, or 5) opposite each of the 100 leader-manager statements on the survey instruments, respondents' scores were subjected to a variety of analyses (see Appendix A). One of the analyses indicated that the study of PLPS data could be based on only 65 of 100 behaviors/functions statements on the survey instruments. That simplifying procedure, in turn, led to a conclusion that only the poles ("leader" and "manager") of the four-category continuum were needed for the analysis that would lead to the substantive findings and to the answers to the research questions, discussed later in this chapter.

Thirty-four of the 65 statements were associated with the leader category (called the Leader-34 scale—see *Table 3-3*) and 31 with the manager category (Manager-31 scale—see *Table 3-4*).

The 34 statements (variables) comprising the Leader-34 scale contain four factors (groupings of variables, with all variables in a given group associated with a particular leader-manager behavior or function—see *Table A-9* in Appendix A). Factor 1 has been labeled "modeling expected behavior." It

91

incorporates such functions as inspiring a shared vision of the future and making clear one's expectation of nondiscriminatory police practices. It also reinforces the need for individual and organizational honesty and integrity, and it suggests that effective leadership relies in large measure on the willingness and ability of the leader to exhibit behavior that is congruent with his or her professed values. Factor 2, "exhibiting interest and concern," underscores the need for leaders to demonstrate that they care about the health, safety, and well-being of the people within their organizations. Factor 3, "serving the community," suggests attention to the agency's superordinate goal and illustrates the ultimate purpose of effective police leadership. Finally, Factor 4, "valuing openness and diversity," challenges the police chief executive to encourage and be attentive to questioning and criticism of agency policies and practices.

The Manager-31 scale was found to contain five factors (the variables composing each factor are noted in *Table A-10* in Appendix A). Factor 1 is "setting standards." It argues that a critically important function of executive management is to ensure that the organization's work is guided by defensible bench marks of competent performance and professional conduct. Factor 2, "keeping promises," is intended to reflect a need for the executive manager to control all aspects of the managerial process, ensuring that agency administrators deliver what they have promised. "Maintaining technical competence" is Factor 3. It means that the organization is managed by people who develop and maintain sufficient technical expertise to manage effectively both present and future organizational conditions. Factor 4, "thinking and behaving rationally," underscores the need for the executive manager's behavioral orientation to be grounded in logic, not emotion. (It does not, however, rule out intuition or creativity in the managerial process.) The rationale behind Factor 5, "demonstrating fiscal responsibility," is self-evident. Big-city policing is an expensive enterprise; its resources must be managed responsibly.

Research Question 1: Big-City Police Chiefs' Professed Values?

The 52 big-city police chiefs who responded to the PLPS expressed a strong belief in the importance of most of the leadership functions in the survey. They indicated, through their responses to the Leader-34 scale variables (listed in *Table 3-7*), a very strong commitment to the kind of purposeful, visionary, and credible leadership that is described in considerable detail in Chapter Two. Although their value commitment to specific management functions of police administration is significantly lower, they also exhibit a keen interest in those tasks and functions (listed in *Table 3-8*) that are distinctly managerial in flavor. That suggests the chiefs believe that whether a particular function is principally oriented toward leadership or toward management, it deserves the *personal* attention of the chief executive.

Leadership. Although there are significant differences among chiefs, their combined PLPS scores reflect solid support for such functions as sharing a vision of the future, encouraging and practicing openness and honesty, developing and challenging employees, creating an atmosphere of teamwork and open communication, helping employees get the job done, and recognizing excellence in performance.

The chiefs also profess a commitment to the following: encouraging questioning and criticism of agency policies; working closely with the communities they serve, which includes a willingness to invite citizen input on policy matters; using an intuitive and creative approach to their work; and standing firm against discriminatory practices.

Management. By comparison, the chiefs *generally* minimize the importance of their personal attention to a variety of managerial functions. They place comparatively little emphasis on such activities as running the organizational meetings that they attend, signing off on agency correspondence, coordinating work flow within the organization, and, generally, controlling the managerial processes within the agency. They particularly reject the idea that they should have more technical expertise than their subordinates, or that they should be able to answer technical questions immediately.

Research Question 2: Distinction in Relative Importance of the Two Functions?

The police chiefs draw a large distinction, at least in theory, between the functions of executive leadership and executive management. Their mean score on the Leader-34 scale (to 1.5) was 4.49; on the Manager-31, it was 3.52, a difference in mean scores significant at the .000 level.[*] (A score of 5 indicates strong agreement regarding performance of the function; a score of 1, strong disagreement.) While the distinction between the two functions is drawn, the evidence is clear that the chiefs also believe that virtually all functions enumerated in the PLPS deserve their personal attention.

Based on median scores on both the Leader-34 and the Manager-31 scales, it was possible to classify each chief as

---

[*] Statistical "significance" can be a confusing term. Put simply, when research reveals a suspected relationship between two variables, an effort is made to determine the extent, if any, to which those variables are related. In the case of our chiefs' expressed beliefs versus their observed behavior, we want to learn whether the differences between the chiefs' responses and the assistants' responses represent a "real" difference or simply a "chance" difference. A difference expressed as "statistically significant" at the .01 level means that there is one chance in 100 that the relationship between the two variables is a chance relationship. That level, incidentally, would indicate a "practical certainty." The higher the number (.10 for example, or a chance factor of 10 in 100), the greater the likelihood that the relationship is only a chance relationship.

scoring "high" or "low" on either or both of the scales of the PLPS. Once the median scores were obtained, all 100 items of the survey (listed in Appendix B) were employed in the analysis, and a single typology was derived. Obviously, there were four possibilities. Presented in *Figure 3-2*, these possibilities include the chiefs who scored (1) high on leadership and low on management; (2) high on leadership and high on management; (3) low on leadership and high on management; and (4) low on leadership and high on management. This typology yields a total of four different orientations to police executive leadership and management. (Note that the median score for the Leader-34 scale was 4.57; for the Manager-31, 3.42.)

Figure 3-2

Crossbreaks Indicating Relationship Between Respondents' Scores on Both the Leader-34 and the Manager-31 Scales: Chiefs Only (N=51)

(1) High Leader, Low Manager	(2) High Leader, High Manager
(4) Low Leader, Low Manager	(3) Low Leader, High Manager

One concern in analyzing and presenting these findings was the possibility that some of the respondents may have simply elected to focus on a particular rating (a "3," for example) and use it as a response pattern in scoring each of the items. That tendency, not uncommon in survey work, might have been expected to surface especially in the scores of the High Leader, High Manager (Type 2) and in the Low Leader, Low Manager (Type 4). An analysis of the four types suggests otherwise.

Each of the types produced responses that ranged at least two position points on the five-point PLPS scale.

Table 3-1 presents the overall findings related to the "leader-manager high-low typology."

Table 3-1
Overall Findings of the Police Executive Leader-Manager High-Low Typology (Chiefs Only)
(N=51)

Type Name	Type Number	Frequency	Valid Percentage
High Leader, Low Manager	1	8	15.7
High Leader, High Manager	2	18	35.3
Low Leader, High Manager	3	8	15.7
Low Leader, Low Manager	4	17	33.3

An examination of the chiefs' responses to specific survey items reveals certain patterns of agreement and disagreement within the four types. Those patterns are presented below.

High Leader, Low Manager (Type 1). All eight chiefs in this category rated 12 PLPS items at the maximum of 5.00 (strong agreement). Those items are identified in *Table 3-2*.

Table 3-2

High-Leader, Low-Manager Responses to the PLPS: Items Achieving Unanimous Agreement at 5.00 (N=8)

Item	Description	Original Scale
13	Addresses each new academy class	L
18	Develops leadership in his/her subordinates	L-M
19	Makes clear expectation for professionalism	M-L
30	Encourages openness and honesty	L-M
41	Acts as model of what is expected of all personnel	L
47	Defines mission and objectives of agency	M-L
53	Recognizes publicly excellent, heroic work	L
54	Is known as one who practices what's preached	L
70	Seen as enthusiastic promoter of agency	L-M
81	Inspires a shared vision of the future	L
86	Encourages initiative throughout the agency	L-M
90	Encourages new ideas by all personnel	L-M

As revealed in *Table 3-2*, the High-Leader, Low-Manager chiefs placed the highest value possible on two of the items within the original manager-leader scales, Items 19 and 47. The full text of Item 19 reads, "Communicates clear expectations for professional conduct of all employees," while the full text of item 47 reads, "Defines the mission and objectives of the agency."

Of the remaining items, excluding those that have been "eliminated," all were found to load within Factor 1 (modeling expected behavior; see *Table A-9*), lending additional strength to the findings of the factor analysis.

At the other extreme of the High-Leader, Low-Manager responses to the PLPS are those items that produced means below the neutral midpoint of "3." These are presented in *Table 3-3*.

Table 3-3

High-Leader, Low-Manager Responses to the PLPS: Items Producing Means of Less Than 3.00 (N=8)

Item	Description	Mean	Original Scale
12	Seen as agency's primary problem solver	2.63	M
15	Runs agency meetings he or she attends	2.88	M-L
20	Spends much time in the office on business	2.63	M
44	Has aide represent at most ceremonial functions	1.88	M
48	Coordinates major activities personally	2.62	M
56	Sets precise work output standards	2.50	M
60	Signs off on all agency correspondence	2.50	M
63	Sets specific objectives for units	2.57	M-L
64	Thoroughly familiar with computer programs	2.75	M
67	Sets, monitors standards for case cancellations	2.80	M-L
68	Has more technical expertise than subordinates	2.25	M
80	Is seen as a good "detail" person	2.88	M
84	Able immediately to answer technical questions	2.50	M
88	Responsible for dispensing drug "buy money"	2.13	M
91	Is responsible for work flow within the agency	2.63	M-L
100	Personally limits, controls overtime expenses	2.63	M

Apparent in the responses reflected in *Table 3-3* is the finding that the High-Leader, Low-Manager chiefs soundly reject the idea that big-city police chiefs should be personally involved in most of the managerial activities of their agencies. However, to learn whether their behavior is consistent with their views, the scores of their assistants were examined. Comparisons are presented in *Table 3-4*, using as a basis scores on the Leader-34, Manager-31 scales. To ensure anonymity, cities are identified by the use of letters.

Table 3-4

Mean Scores of the High-Leader, Low-Manager Chiefs and Their Assistants on the Leader-34, Manager-31 Scales
(N=8)

| City | Leader-34 | | Manager-31 | |
	Chief	Assistant	Chief	Assistant
A	4.88	4.82	3.13	3.90
B	4.62	4.65	3.29	3.83
C	4.76	2.41	3.13	2.55
D	4.59	4.88	3.29	3.94
E	4.76	3.71	3.26	2.89
F	4.70	4.34	3.23	3.85
G	4.88	3.85	3.32	3.32
H	4.59	3.44	2.65	3.30

As seen in *Table 3-4*, High-Leader, Low-Manager chiefs are given high marks by their assistants in about half the cases on the Leader-34 scale; in two instances, the assistants rate their chiefs even higher on the leadership scale than do their bosses themselves. Conversely, on the Manager-31 scale, most ratings reflect a belief on the part of the assistants that their bosses are more involved in the management arena than the chiefs themselves believe is appropriate. (Further analysis revealed that a total of 13.5 percent of the assistants viewed their bosses as High-Leader, Low-Manager chiefs; the figure for the High-Leader, High-Manager chiefs was 34.8 percent, for the Low-Leader, High-Manager it was 15.7 percent, and for the Low-Leader, Low-Manager, the figure was 36 percent.)

High Leader, High Manager (Type 2). With a sample of more than twice the numbers of High-Leader, Low-Manager chiefs, the High-Leader, High-Manager group produced maximum 5.00 scores on 10 of the PLPS items. Only three items were rated at less than the neutral midpoint. They are Item 44 (has aide represent at most ceremonial functions); Item 68 (has more technical expertise than subordinates); and Item 88 (responsible for dispensing drug "buy money"), all from the original manager scale.

Low Leader, High Manager (Type 3). The Low-Leader, High-Manager chiefs did not record combined 5.00 scores. The closest they came was 4.88 on three items, each of which has at its core a commitment to honesty and integrity: Item 30 (encourages openness and honesty), Item 54 (is known as one who practices what's preached), and Item 74 (seen by employees as absolutely honest).

Seven of this group's responses fell below the neutral mid-point; only three were from the original leader or leader-manager scales.

Low Leader, Low Manager (Type 4). Not surprisingly the overall scores of the Low-Leader, Low-Manager chiefs are quite low. The highest rating, 4.88, was for Item 19 (makes clear expectation for professionalism). The lowest, 1.59, was for Item 68 (has more technical expertise than subordinates).

Research Question 3: Chiefs' Behavior Consistent With Professed Values?

According to their immediate assistants, the behavior of chiefs is not consistent with the values they expressed on the PLPS. This is particularly true of the Leader-34 scale, where the difference between professed values and observed behavior was significant at the .000 level. While the assistants generally view their bosses as honest, open to public and employee input and criticism, clear about their expectations of nondis-criminatory police practices, and skilled in internal and external politics, they are much less inclined to describe their chiefs' behavior as congruent with most other values embedded in the Leader-34 scale.

The gap between the chiefs' opinions and the assistants' observations was considerably narrower on the Manager-31 scale, although it was significant at .01 level. The findings here also make clear that what the chiefs profess to value is, in many respects, inconsistent with their observed behavior. They are seen, for example, as much more technically competent than they themselves believe chiefs ought to be. Their subordinates report that, contrary to the chiefs' responses, their bosses run the meetings that they attend, spend much time in the office attending to the business of the agency, and personally control the key managerial processes of the organization. The chiefs are seen, moreover, as having more technical expertise than their subordinates and able to answer immediately most questions from their subordinates or their own superiors.

Mean scores and standard deviations for the Leader-34 and Manager-31 scales were calculated for each group of respondents: the chiefs and the assistants. That was followed by an analysis of variance[*], which led to a finding of the degree of significance in the differences between the responses of the chiefs versus the assistants. The data are presented first for the Leader-34 scale, then for the Manager-31 scale.

As will be made clear, both the chiefs and the assistants draw a very clear distinction between the police agency's leadership functions and its management functions.

The chiefs' mean score on the Leader-34 scale (*Table 3-3*) was 4.49, while the assistants' average score on the same scale was 4.12 (*Table 3-5*). This difference is significant at the .000 level and suggests that chiefs did not behave in the leadership arena in accordance with their own values. They attached a

---

*Like the standard deviation, but computed differently, variance measures the average dispersion about the mean. The smaller the variance, the more closely grouped are the variables' values about their mean.

higher priority to the concepts of leadership than they were apparently willing or able to exhibit behaviorally.

Table 3-5

Breakdown of PLPS Scores on the Leader-34 Scale: Chiefs Versus Assistants

	Mean	SD	F-ratio	Sig.
Chiefs (N=52)	4.49	.35	14.37	.000
Assistants (N=89)	4.12	.64		

For the Manager-31 scale (*Table 3-4*) the chiefs' mean score was 3.52 and the assistants' was 3.71 (*Table 3-6*), a difference that is statistically significant at the .08 level. Such a difference indicates that chiefs were significantly more involved in the managerial processes of their organizations than their own values suggested they ought to be.

Table 3-6

Breakdown of PLPS Scores on the Manager-31 Scale: Chiefs Versus Assistants

	Mean	SD	F-ratio	Sig.
Chiefs (N=51)	3.52	.60	3.11	.080
Assistants (N=91)	3.71	.60		

The presentation of more detailed findings is necessary in order to learn exactly where the chiefs' views and their own behaviors may or may not coincide. To this end, a further breakdown reflecting differences and similarities in responses to the two PLPS scales is presented in *Tables 3-7* and *3-8*. Those tables offer chief and assistant responses to variables in the Leader-34 and Manager-31 scales. Significance is designated as follows: .01 = *; .001 = **; .000 = ***; or, not significant = NS. (The higher the significance level, the more likely that the differences between chiefs' and assistants' responses are due to chance. A significance level of .01 indicates "a practical certainty" that differences are not due to chance.) The number of cases varies from 143 to 144 throughout the data, with 52 chiefs and 91 or 92 assistants responding to each variable.

The leadership findings. In *Table 3-7* the differences between the chiefs' responses and those of their assistants on the Leader-34 scale of the PLPS are statistically significant for 18 items, over half the variables. In each of those instances, chiefs scored higher on the variable than did assistants. That may mean that the chiefs place a much higher value on these functions or dimensions of police leadership than their assistants would attribute to their chiefs based on observations.

Sixteen of the statistically significant variables of the Leader-34 are grouped within Factor 1 (modeling expected behavior; see *Table A-9* in Appendix A). The other two statistically significant variables— "Wears the agency's uniform periodically" and "Sends cards to injured or ill employees" belong to Factor 2 (exhibiting interest and concern). The Factor 1 variables reflect an emphasis on such leadership functions as sharing a vision of the future, encouraging and practicing openness and honesty, developing and challenging employees, creating an atmosphere of teamwork and open communication, helping employees get the job done, and recognizing excellence in performance.

Table 3-7

Leader-34 Scale: Chiefs' Versus Assistants' Mean Responses

		Mean Scores		
Item	Description	Chiefs	Assistants	Sig.
1	Encourages questioning, criticism	4.00	3.97	NS
2	Facilitates work of agency employees	4.58	4.25	*
5	Invites citizen input on agency policies	3.96	3.96	NS
6	Challenges people to do better	4.75	4.26	**
10	Develops leadership capabilities in others	4.79	4.08	***
13	Addresses each new academy class	4.50	4.57	NS
14	Makes clear expectations of performance	4.70	4.12	***
18	Develops responsibility in subordinates	4.81	4.17	***
21	Meets often with community leaders	4.37	4.25	NS
22	Is open to community feedback	4.56	4.33	NS
25	Approaches work intuitively, creatively	4.35	4.05	NS
26	Enlists support in setting objectives	4.75	4.21	***
29	Visits families of slain, injured officers	4.70	4.38	NS
30	Encourages openness, honesty	4.90	4.55	*
33	Builds team spirit, teamwork	4.70	3.86	***
34	Develops, encourages use of "open door"	4.35	4.14	NS
41	Acts as model of expected behavior	4.56	4.15	*
42	Elicits feedback on policies, practices	4.60	4.05	**
45	Wears the uniform periodically	3.94	3.18	*
49	Celebrates accomplishments of workers	4.35	4.15	NS
50	Uses all means to communicate	4.56	3.86	***
53	Publicly recognizes fine, heroic work	4.85	4.59	*
54	Practices what he or she preaches	4.73	4.35	*
57	Shares true feelings about agency issues	4.29	3.96	NS
58	Is clear on nondiscrimination policy	4.70	4.56	NS
61	Attends many community meetings	4.09	4.21	NS
65	Sends cards to injured or ill employees	3.96	3.30	*
69	Places high value on diversity of opinion	3.96	3.77	NS
73	Visits hospitalized members	4.02	3.95	NS
74	Seen by employees as absolutely honest	4.75	4.54	NS
81	Inspires shared vision of future	4.65	4.01	***
86	Encourages initiative throughout agency	4.63	4.12	**
90	Encourages new ideas by all employees	4.71	4.23	**
97	Masters internal, external politics	4.46	4.23	NS

Symbol		Significance Level
*	=	<.01
**	=	<.001
***	=	<.000
NS	=	Not significant

The findings suggest that the chiefs value those functions to a significantly greater degree than they are observed to practice them.

The analysis of variance supports these findings. For example, the chiefs place a very high value (4.70) on Item 33 of the PLPS, "Builds a strong sense of team spirit and teamwork throughout the agency." As noted in *Table 3-3*, the assistants give their bosses a rating of 3.86 on this variable. The difference is significant at the .000 level. Similarly, high F-ratios[*] were recorded for many other variables. Some examples include "Works to develop leadership capabilities throughout the supervisory ranks" (25.36); "Develops in his or her subordinates a strong sense of personal responsibility for good work" (23.31); "Uses all available means to communicate with employees at all levels" (21.61); "Makes clear his or her personal expectations for effective performance" (18.26); "Challenges people in the organization to do better" (16.86); "Enlists the support of others in setting agency objectives" (16.43); and "Inspires throughout the organization a shared vision of the future" (15.63).

On the other hand, many of the variables that produced no statistically significant differences between the scores of the chiefs and those of their assistants are worth highlighting. For example, the assistants observe in their bosses' behavior, to a degree roughly equivalent to what the chiefs themselves profess, the encouragement of questioning and criticism of agency policies; a strong dedication to the communities they serve, which includes a willingness to invite citizen input on

---

*If the F-ratio has a value of 1 or less, significant variation does not exist between what is being compared. Since the F-ratios reported above are well in excess of 1, that suggests that the difference between PLPS scores recorded by the chiefs and those recorded by assistants are significant. The higher the F-ratio, the less the chance that the researcher's statement or conclusion is indefensible.

policy matters; an intuitive and creative approach to their work; and a firm stand against discriminatory practices.

Finally, there are some ambiguous findings. The chiefs and assistants were found to agree on three variables that are closely related to items that produced statistically significant differences. They are Item 49 (celebrates the accomplishments of employees), which seems to conflict with the results on Item 53 (recognizes publicly the excellent and/or heroic work of employees); Item 57 (shares with others in the organization his or her true feelings about agency issues), possibly in conflict with Item 30 scores (encourages openness and honesty throughout the organization); and Item 74 (is seen by his or her employees as absolutely honest), which also seems to conflict with the disparate scores on Item 30 and with Item 54 (is known as one who practices what he or she preaches).

The management findings. As seen in *Table 3-8*, the managerial functions of the police chiefs' professional world generated far fewer statistically significant differences between the chiefs and their assistants. In fact, only six of the variables of the Manager-31 scale achieved statistical significance. None of the six is in Factor 1 (setting standards) of the Manager-31 scale; three are in Factor 2 (keeping promises; items 15, 20, and 76) and three are in Factor 3 (maintaining technical competence; 28, 68, and 84).

Also apparent from the findings in *Table 3-8* is that in each instance of a statistically significant difference between the chiefs' values and their observed behavior, the chiefs scored lower than their assistants, meaning that they apparently place less value on the managerial functions. That finding is precisely the reverse of the finding on the Leader-34 scale, in which the chiefs scored themselves higher on each leadership variable than did their assistants.

Table 3-8
Manager-31 Scale: Chiefs' Versus Assistants' Mean Responses

		Means		
Item	Description	Chiefs	Assistants	Sig.
4	Intimately involved in budget	4.15	4.08	NS
11	Personally sets agency priorities	3.90	4.16	NS
12	Seen as agency's problem solver	3.15	3.54	NS
15	Runs meetings he/she attends	3.41	4.26	***
16	Maintains control at all times	3.75	4.10	NS
20	Spends much time in the office	3.13	4.14	***
24	Intimately familiar with the law	3.65	3.73	NS
27	Intimately involved in planning	4.19	4.10	NS
28	Able to answer boss's questions now	3.79	4.34	***
32	Constantly up to date on budget	4.17	4.22	NS
36	Known as effective organizer	3.90	3.83	NS
39	Personally monitors per capita costs	3.12	3.44	NS
43	Knows at all times what is going on	3.79	3.80	NS
48	Coordinates major activities of agency	3.15	3.56	NS
52	Seen as neutral, objective manager	4.13	3.82	NS
56	Sets precise work output standards	3.50	3.21	NS
60	Signs off on all correspondence	2.90	2.98	NS
63	Sets specific objectives for units	3.48	3.49	NS
67	Sets norms, monitors case cancellations	3.04	2.67	NS
68	Has more technical expertise	2.25	2.90	*
72	Is logical, orderly, unemotional	3.92	4.04	NS
75	Personally directs subordinates' work	3.51	3.56	NS
76	Controls key managerial processes	3.39	3.96	**
79	Enforces chain of command	3.58	3.43	NS
80	Seen as good "detail" person	3.15	3.57	NS
84	Able to answer technical questions now	2.77	3.69	***
87	Personally works on agency policies	4.10	4.24	NS
91	Responsible for work flow	2.90	2.89	NS
95	Responsible for resource allocation	4.02	4.12	NS
96	Sets unequivocal lines of authority	4.13	3.92	NS
100	Sets limits for, controls overtime	3.08	2.99	NS

Symbol		Significance Level
*	=	<.01
**	=	<.001
***	=	<.000
NS	=	Not significant

As with certain of the Leader-34 variables, the Manager-31 scale produced several large discrepancies between what the chiefs profess to value and what their subordinates report they observe in the behavior of their bosses. While the two groups are much more closely aligned in their observations and opinions (the Manager-31 scale having produced only one-third the number of variables with statistically significant differences than were found on the Leader-34 scale), those differences that do exist are quite large.

For example, Item 15 (runs agency meetings that he or she attends), statistically significant at the .000 level, produced the highest F-ratio (.38) of any other variable in either of the scales. The police chiefs apparently place relatively little emphasis on the practice of running meetings; their mean score was 3.41. But their assistants, with a mean of 4.26, report that the practice among their superiors is apparently quite common.

Item 20 (also significant at the .000 level), "Spends as much time as possible in the office, attending to the business of the agency," produced an F-ratio of .31. Again, the chiefs give this practice one of their lowest ratings (3.13); yet, their assistants maintain that this behavior is also common (4.14).

Item 84, "Is able to answer immediately most work-related technical questions," produced among the chiefs their fourth lowest score of the entire survey (2.77). Yet, to a statistically significant level of .000, their subordinates maintain that the chiefs are, in fact, able to answer immediately most technical questions about their work. The F-ratio on Item 84 is 25.50. Item 28, a similar variable, "Is able to answer immediately questions from his or her boss(es) about police operations," found the chiefs and their assistants differing again at the .000 level of significance. The F-ratio here is 14.07.

Whether the chiefs "Personally [control] the key managerial processes of the agency" is the subject of Item 76. The chiefs indicate significantly less desire for, or preoccupation with, personal control over the managerial processes of their agencies than they are observed by their assistants to actually exert. The F-ratio here is .11.

Finally, the chiefs place very little value for leadership purposes in having more technical expertise than their subordinates (Item 68). However, their immediate subordinates report that their bosses do indeed have more technical expertise than their employees. The F-ratio on Item 68 is 9.86.

Research Question 4: Differences Based on Demographics?

As of the date of the PLPS, America's big-city police chiefs were exclusively male, predominantly white, and in their early fifties. On average, they had 16.4 years of education, were in police work 26.6 years, and headed their agencies for 4.1 years. They served populations ranging from 208,000 to 4.3 million with organizations that ranged from 359 employees to 10,590. Slightly more than 64 percent of the agencies are decentralized.

Given the major differences in demographic characteristics, both individual and contextual, one might expect that the PLPS would produce significantly different responses based on these variables. Such was not the case.

Regarding chiefs who are Type 1 (High Leader, Low Manager—see above discussion of research question number 2), they came from moderately populated newer cities of the sun belt that cover substantially more square miles than other cities of the study.

The promise of confidentiality precludes identification of those cities, but it may be reported that they are generally without the history of institutionalized corruption that has characterized policing in the older cities. Moreover, the other chiefs head agencies that are at least twice the size of theirs, suggesting that the High-Leader, Low-Manager chiefs are not faced with the problems of densely populated urban centers or of massive police bureaucracies.

Further, as can be seen in *Table 3-9*, the High-Leader, Low-Manager chiefs are significantly the most highly educated. They are also the youngest. Finally, they have been the chief executive of their agencies for less than half the time of their colleagues.

Table 3-9

Individual and Contextual Characteristics of the Chiefs on the Police Executive Leader-Manager High-Low Typology: Mean Scores (Chiefs Only) (N=51)

Type	Years of Education	Age	Years in Policing	Years as Chief	City Rank	Square Miles	Sworn Personnel
1	17.63	48.00	25.31	1.31	48	187	686
2	15.50	50.81	24.37	3.91	37	159	1409
3	16.25	53.14	31.98	4.59	41	137	1542
4	17.00	49.59	26.91	5.08	45	140	1080

While certain trends in the data suggest that chiefs who are younger, less tenured as chiefs, more highly educated, and who head the smallest and youngest of the big-city agencies are more likely to emerge as those with the strongest leader orientations, this cannot be concluded here. It is true that two statistically significant[*] demographic correlations were produced. One is in the relationship between education and the managerial orientation (the less educated, the more managerial) and the other is in the relationship between time in policing and the leadership orientation (the less time, the stronger the leadership orientation). However, caution is in

---

*See previous footnote on significance level.

order. When the scores of chiefs who scored high on the Leader-34 scale and low on the Manager-31 scales are compared with the scores of their own subordinates, only half of the chiefs are described by their assistants as behaving in a manner consistent with their professed commitment to the leadership values. Furthermore, the population of those chiefs is so small (eight) that any generalization would be risky.

The safe conclusion is that the relationship between demographic characteristics and the police chiefs' leadership and management attitudes and behavior is relatively weak. Apparently, the homogeneity of the police culture serves to produce remarkably similar views of the organizational and community concerns presented in the PLPS.

One thing, however, does seem certain: it is much easier to embrace—and presumably to practice—important leadership principles in a conducive setting. A conducive setting, based on the results of the research, is one in which the city policed is comparatively young, large in square miles, and small in population.

Chapter Four

ESSENTIAL QUALITIES OF THE POLICE LEADER

Throughout this study, particularly in Chapters One and Two, much has been made of the difficulty of contemporary big-city police work: high rates of crime and violence and other social conditions that make policing a dangerous and, to some, an unpopular job; a painful history as a social institution; public criticism of and ambivalence toward police or support tendered only during times of crisis; and conditions of work and aspects of organizational structure and culture that conspire to (1) frustrate crime-fighting effectiveness and responsive police service and (2) create psychologically destructive tendencies among police officers. Those are some of the conditions that form the leadership challenge for America's big-city police departments.

Leading the Police

One thing is certain: As difficult as police work is today, it will be more so in the future (Tafoya, 1986).[*] This reality raises key questions about the fundamental orientation of big-city police chiefs. There is substantial evidence (Chapter Two) that many in leadership positions exhibit a cautious and reactive orientation. Their motive base is essentially directed toward avoiding mistakes, maintaining the status quo. This orientation, contrasted against a more creative approach to organizational leadership, undoubtedly works against not only

---

[*]Tafoya, supervisory special agent with the FBI, wrote his doctoral dissertation on the future of policing. His study, which took the form of Delphi research, produced a mixed but generally troubling forecast.

113

the police chiefs' success as leaders but also their professional survival as well.

Life and Death in Police Work

Addressing himself to the distinction between the two orientations, creative versus reactive, Stern (1967:165) comments on Heidegger's philosophy of life:

> Requesting that man live "authentically," by expecting his death at any moment and considering anxiety of death as the criterion of a life's "authenticity" (*Eigentlichkeit*), Heidegger places our whole life under the dominion of death. His philosophy is one of *memento mori*. Such a philosophy might be fit for monks who sleep every night in their coffins and who, in life, have nothing to do but to prepare themselves for death. However, applied to the secular life, Heidegger's philosophy of *memento mori* would mean the end of any creative existence. If we want to perform great deeds in life, we must live under the fiction of immortality.

Stern's suggestion that greatness requires one to function under the illusion of everlasting life would likely be met with great cynicism and derision by many in the police field. Theirs is a world where possibility of sudden, violent death is always present.[*] But Stern's counsel is consistent with much of the work of those who examine the spiritual side of the leadership challenge (see especially McKnight, 1984). It is aligned also

---

*It is important to note at this late stage that police officer mortality rates are considerably lower than those of many other occupations. In fact, during the decade of the 1970s officer slayings averaged slightly over 114 per year (Blumberg and Niederhoffer, 1985), making police work safer than mining, agriculture, fire fighting, construction, and several other occupations. That death toll has risen to about 153 deaths per year in the 1980s. What cannot be overlooked, however, is that many officers lose their lives in gun battles and other forms of criminal violence, the likes of which produce in the police culture a healthy respect for what Skolnick called the "symbolic assailant" (Skolnick, 1966).

with those variables of the PLPS that look to the future (e.g., Item 81: inspires throughout the organization a shared vision of the future). Given the truncated tenure of most big-city police chiefs, it would seem to be imperative that these leaders approach their work *as if* they are going to be in the leadership position long enough to make a difference. Perhaps that attitude might help make it so.

Visionary Leadership

It is unlikely that leaders with a reactive orientation to their lives would ever move beyond the development of organizational "goals" and "objectives" to the kind of uplifting, passionate sentiments found increasingly in the vision statements of a variety of organizations (Kouzes and Posner, 1987; Ouchi, 1981), statements that project the organization into the future and that reflect a deep commitment to the service ideal.

Block maintains that "[n]ot just any vision will do...it needs to be...lofty in order to capture our imagination and engage our spirit" (1987:102). Big-city policing presents a particularly fertile ground for the development of such a vision statement. The job of the urban cop, for all its trials, its moments of anger, pain, and frustration, offers intrinsic satisfactions denied people in many other lines of work. Stopping someone from hurting another is one such intrinsic satisfaction. So is catching a bank robber, providing comfort to those who have been traumatized by an automobile accident, a crib death, a neighborhood or family disturbance, or a missing child.

Policing is a most direct and potentially deeply satisfying form of service. It is intrinsically noble and honorable work, and yet account after account in the literature presents the street officer's point of view in less than flattering terms. Recall that, for many cops, police work is "asshole control" and dealing with "shitheads" (Manning and Van Maanen, 1978).

115

Police executives occupy critically important positions of influence in the lives of their officers. It is argued that one of the most useful things they can do for their officers and, consequently, for their communities is to invite those who do the work to participate in a process of developing a shared vision for the organization. A vision statement answers the question what do we really want for the organization, for the community? Put differently, what do we stand for, what do we believe in?

The San Diego Police Department, while developing its statement at the command staff level (essentially captains and up), has nonetheless taken a large step in the right direction. It has articulated a vision for the future that, if handled well, has the potential for empowering present and future members of the organization to do increasingly more effective work and to derive increasingly greater satisfaction from that work. Among other things, it has taken to calling itself "America's Finest" police department. It challenges, in the process, other law enforcement agencies to prove they are better. In a day when "We're No Worse Than Anyone Else" is only half-jokingly suggested as a slogan for beleaguered organizations, the pride implicit in San Diego's approach is refreshing indeed.

In any event, if it is true as suggested by Bass (1985) that the leader's principal function is to structure organizational expectations, the development, crystallization, and continuing reinforcement of a vision statement can serve as a powerful device to that end. Big-city policing, it is argued, is in desperate need of something good to believe in.

Why not create it? Why not *envision* big-city policing as a respected and respectable social institution? Why not picture the work being performed by exceptionally effective crime fighters, police officers who, having committed themselves to being competent at what they have been hired to do, have organized and mobilized the community in responsible crime prevention programs? Why not look into the future and see police officers who are terrifically adept at detecting and apprehending criminal offenders, especially violent, predatory types? And why not see officers who, through the quality of their crime scene protection, their investigative prowess, and their professional testimony in court, assist in the successful prosecution of criminal offenders?

Why not create a vision of police officers who provide dignified and respectful services to all citizens—and noncitizens—such that the officers come to be appreciated, not merely needed by the community? Why not see police work that is practiced in an enlightened, nondiscriminatory fashion by officers who are socially aware, fully informed of the delicacy of their role, and whose everyday practices reject unethical conduct in any form, including racism, sexism, and any other manifestation of human bigotry?

Why not choose to see police work that has been made as safe as police work can be made?

Why not envision police officers enjoying themselves, engaged in a labor of love, working for bosses who care about their physical and emotional health and well-being, bosses who set and enforce reasonable, job-related, and nondiscriminatory standards of performance and conduct, bosses who recognize and reward exceptional performance and who are likewise quick to deal with employees whose performance or conduct is unacceptable?

Finally, why not choose to see police work guided and directed by executives who set the proper tone for all of this to happen, who work to create an organizational climate that supports this kind of police work?

For the cynic, such vision statements are mere pipe dreams. They are inspired by a myopic, totally unrealistic view of the real world. And they are dangerous, particularly when

117

embraced by leaders in positions of power and authority. They have the effect of raising expectations, expectations that cannot possibly be met because of conditions contained in the *current reality*.

Yet it is precisely because of problems in the current reality, argue some observers (Kiefer and Senge, 1984; Kiefer and Stroh, 1984; Ross, 1987), that it is important to stake out a desirable place in the future, to envision the world as one wants it to be. This, rather than creating unrealistic expectations, has the effect of creating a healthy structural tension between one's current reality and his or her vision. Influenced by Sartre (see Stern, 1967), Forrester (1981), and others, these thinkers believe strongly in the necessity for the leader to be firmly grounded in the current reality. Indeed, their suggestion is that through development of *personal mastery* (Fritz, 1984), one can hold in mind concurrently one's vision of the future and his or her conception of the current reality. The tension created thereby is experienced as a creative energy serving to motivate the individual—or the organization—in the direction of the vision.

Kouzes and Posner write, "The vision of a leader is the magnetic north that sets the compass course of the company. We want to have it described to us in rich detail so that we will know when we have arrived and so that we can select the proper route for getting there" (1987:20). This makes clear a belief that, while leadership is a process, it is also a journey with a destination. The police chief executive who, along with members of his or her agency, creates a vision for the future is also making a promise of arrival.

Serving Others

There is another strong, unmistakable philosophical theme to the work of fine leaders. Kouzes and Posner (1987) found it in leaders they studied and called it the "socialized power

118

concern." Contrasting the socialized power concern against the personalized power concern (displayed, for example, in the form of rudeness, excessive drinking, sexual exploitation of others, ostentatious cars, fancy offices), Kouzes and Posner argue that truly effective leaders have a genuine desire to be of service to others.

Burns is but one of a growing number of observers to argue that leaders should be of service not only to their constituents (or their clientele or their customers) but to their employees as well. His call for transformational leadership is quite explicit: the leader should devote himself or herself to the transformation of followers into leaders. This means, among other things, that the leader must serve the followers, must be in touch with their needs, their hopes and aspirations, their fears. By doing so, maintains Burns, leaders "serve as an *independent force in changing the makeup of the followers' motive base through gratifying their motives*" (1978:20).

The PLPS presented several opportunities to test the police chiefs' commitment to service, both to the community and to their employees. Unfortunately, there was a large, statistically significant gap between professed values and observed behavior in several key areas relating to the executives' service orientation. Highly significant, for example, were Item 10 (develops leadership capabilities in others), Item 18 (develops responsibility in subordinates), and Item 33 (builds team spirit and teamwork). Somewhat less significant was Item 2 (facilitates the work of agency employees).

One of the best indications of the priorities of a leader is how he or she spends his or her time. Kouzes and Posner (1987:180) contend that "[t]he most genuine way to demonstrate that you really care and are concerned about other people as human beings is to spend time with them." They go on to suggest that leaders should schedule their work to permit informal contact with employees on a daily basis.

119

Of course, the quality of time is also important. Jablin (1982) found in their studies that the quality of interaction with one's boss is actually more important than the quantity. In any event, the PLPS offers substantial evidence that big-city police chiefs, while they profess to value the quality in leaders, spend very little of their time with their own personnel, learning what their employees need and servicing those needs.

Burns (1978:20), lest there be any misunderstanding of the nature of the leader's service orientation, offers this:

> Leaders and followers may be inseparable in function, but they are not the same. The leader takes the initiative in making the leader-led connection; it is the leader who creates the links that allow communication and exchange to take place.

Leader as Model

Item 41 of the PLPS was conceived as a crucial leadership variable. The full text reads, "Acts as a model of what is expected of all personnel." French and Raven (1959) identified "referent" power as one of the most potent forces of influence in an organization, and Kouzes and Posner (1987:190) argue that "Leaders provide the standard by which other people in the organization calibrate their own choices and behaviors. In order to set an example, leaders must know their values and live them." The chiefs obviously strongly agreed with this premise when they accorded Item 41 a value of 4.56. Once again, however, a significant difference is found between what they believe to be important and how they actually behave.

Earlier in this study (Chapter Two) the point is made that leaders, as well as their followers, are subjected to enormously powerful influences of organizational structure and organizational culture. There is, however, a strong case to be made for individual responsibility and individual choice. Block (1987) stresses the power of "fundamental choices" that leaders can make. They take the form of deciding between maintenance and greatness, between caution and courage, and between dependency and autonomy. While the forces of structure are strong, "A person, whether leader or follower, girded with moral purpose is a tiny principality of power" (Burns, 1978:457).

The police chiefs, having chosen to accept responsibility for the quality of organizational life within the department and for police practices in the community, have also, it is argued, accepted responsibility for knowing and understanding the nature and the conditions of the work, providing powerful and purposeful leadership that at once guides and *serves* the work force and behaving as a model of what is expected of all agency personnel.

Leadership Qualities

Much of the literature on organizational leadership addresses the question of needed or desirable leader qualities (see especially Bass, 1981). Implicit in both the items themselves and in the responses to the PLPS are such leader qualities. Some are generic and would likely appear on any list of leader qualities; others may offer, if only by emphasis, special utility for the police chief executive.

Credibility

Important to note at once is that *followers* ultimately determine the appropriateness or the desirability of leader qualities and leader behavior. Another way of putting this is to suggest that one's "effort to change the behavior of others is *attempted* leadership" (Bass, 1960, cited in Bass, 1981:10). If the chief executives are to function as more than putative leaders of the police organization, they must exert true influence on the behavior of their subordinates.

There is good reason to believe that the big-city police chiefs will not be able to exert the desired leadership influence unless they thoroughly understand—and convincingly communicate their understanding of—the nature of the work. This familiarity must extend to the police culture itself. Established in Chapter Two is evidence of the social isolation that police officers experience as a result of several conditions of the work: danger (including the "symbolic assailant") authority, in-group solidarity (Skolnick, 1966), and police cynicism (Blumberg and Niederhoffer, 1985). The occupation's socialization and acculturation of police officers exerts a remarkably powerful influence on their lives and creates a unique "police mentality." The police chiefs must know and understand this mentality if they are to enjoy credibility among those whose behavior is shaped by it.

Edward R. Murrow, talking about journalists and news commentators, once said, "To be persuasive we must be believable; to be believable we must be credible; to be credible, we must be truthful" (Kouzes and Posner, 1987:15). Quite apart from one's standing as the "top cop" of the police organization with whatever credibility that gives the police chief, that dimension of credibility called truthfulness must be addressed. Police officers work in a world where cheating, stealing, and lying are everyday occurrences. They are trained to "smell" a lie, conditioned to be suspicious of people's statements and their motives. While the destructive personal effects of this everyday reality of work are well documented and properly bemoaned, it remains a fact of life. And police chiefs risk much if they lie to their officers. Absolute honesty in one's dealings with everyone under all circumstances is a good rule for police chiefs to follow. While difficult to imagine this rule being followed by chief executives in any line of work—absolute is absolute—it is encouraging to note no significant difference between the chiefs and the assistants' responses to Item 74 (is seen by his or her employees as absolutely honest).

It is also wise for big-city police chiefs to exhibit unimpeachable personal integrity. Mixed signals, broken promises, or other indications of a lack of harmony between what is said and what is done by police chiefs result in an erosion of their power as leaders. On the apparent premise that most leaders are well intentioned and have socially desirable ends in mind, Block defines integrity as "our willingness to live out our vision, even against all odds."

This research has produced evidence of an integrity problem in big-city policing. The overall results, concluding that there is a significant difference between what the chiefs value and what they practice, are reason enough for the statement. Evidence suggests that America's big-city police chiefs need to examine very carefully (1) what they have promised their organizations explicitly or implicitly and (2) what they have delivered. Better by far is a conclusion of this research that the chiefs not inspire hope in the first place if they have not the material means, the will, or the personal ability to make it happen.

Love

Another quality believed to be critical to the cause of powerful police leadership is that of love. Leadership is generally conceded to be an affair of the heart rather than the head. And in police work, given the fear, the frustration, the brutishness, and the pathos that constitute inevitable moments of the practice, the agency's leader ought to have a transcendent love for the work—as it is and as it can be—as well as for the people who do it. Love cannot be faked. Cops will see through the disingenuous leader.

Other Qualities

There are, of course, other qualities that the effective leader must possess. As one studies the Leader-34 functions of the

PLPS, these qualities come to mind: an appropriately tough and demanding nature, with a demonstrated ability to set and enforce reasonable standards of employee performance and conduct; fairness; an abiding commitment to justice in all arenas; energy and a willingness to invest large amounts of time in both the organizational and the community settings; verbal fluency and persuasiveness; interpersonal skills, including active listening and a willingness to engage in constructive confrontation; maturity and patience; an appreciation of differences among people, as well as a tolerance for the ambiguity that is an ever-present condition of policing; political mastery; and the kind of perseverance that is necessary to meet the demands of a reasoned and responsible police practice day in and day out.

Finally, the modern police leader must have a strong future-oriented, systems-thinking bias if he or she is to be successful. Even a cursory examination of both the Leader-34 and Manager-31 functions makes clear the complexity and the inherent contradictions of the work of big-city police chief executives. Bass (1985) calls it "structuring expectations," while Schein (1985) argues that it is "embedding culture," but "it" is the primary work of leadership and getting it accomplished requires a solid foundation of knowledge, skills, and the temperament necessary to understand and guide credibly the complex organism known as the police bureaucracy.

As a postscript to this discussion on the leadership qualities of the police chief, it is important to take note once again of the demographic characteristics of the country's big-city police leaders. At the time of the PLPS, there was not a woman among them at the chief level; only 3 percent of the assistants were women (many in nonsworn positions, making them effectively ineligible for promotion to the top spot). Blacks constituted only 6 percent of the chiefs and a little over 9 percent of the assistants. Slightly under 10 percent of the chiefs were

Hispanic, and only 2.3 percent of the assistants. The combined Asian population stood at 1.4 percent, and the American Indian population was also very small.

Full representation of women and ethnic minorities in the leadership ranks of American police departments ought not to be viewed solely as a legal and a moral obligation. The institution needs the voices of a culturally diverse group of leaders and managers in such areas as policy making, problem solving, crisis management, and program development. Such diversity provides a range of information and a richness of perspective that urban policing sorely needs. Further, as long as police executive leadership remains virtually the exclusive domain of the white male, it will stand as a mockery of local officials' efforts at representative government.

Prospects of Change

Assuming that the police chief executive perceives a need to change his or her approach to leadership, what are the prospects? Most social and behavioral scientists offer little hope for optimism. Indeed, the very assumption that a significant number of leaders might be interested in changing their leadership practices needs to be examined. Warren Bennis reported to Ghiselin (1987a:8–9) in an interview that

> Freud said that each of us was three: id, ego, and superego, or ambition, competence, and conscience. In this narcissistic world, id seems to be all. Our ambition, our greed has killed off our conscience and made competence irrelevant. I guess my gloomy sense of where we are today is that I see too much of the ambition and not enough of the combination.
>
> Instead of leaders, we have celebrities, stars, heroes. We even have McHeroes, those pseudo-stars the media cranks out in

extraordinary numbers for our momentary delectation.

While Bennis's outlook may seem unduly pessimistic—indeed the researcher's own experience in the field suggests that most police leaders care deeply about the quality of leadership within the profession—it does point up the challenge of change facing the individual leader. It may be recalled that Goldstein (1977) warned against the colorful, charismatic leader who is effective at deflecting attention away from the substance of leadership by concentrating on its "appearance," a phenomenon analyzed by Goffman (1959). It is unlikely that such individuals would be motivated to change, short of some catalytic event that requires them to do so.

In any event, the issue is not personality transformation of police leaders, it is the need for a critical examination of their executive leadership behavior. Wheelis (1973:101) notes that "we are what we do," and if having examined our practices, "we want to change what we are, we must begin by changing what we do, must undertake a new mode of action. Since the import of such action is change, it will run afoul of existing entrenched forces which will protest and resist." Wheelis, then, provides more evidence of the difficulty of personal change.

But it can be done, and on the basis of the results of the PLPS, it is argued that for some the change is urgently needed. Once again, the call for change is not directed at the chiefs' values (they are inspirational) or their personalities (most chief executives in this researcher's experience are at least pleasant) or their motives (they clearly want what is best for their communities and for their organizations). Instead, the call for change is directed at those structures and those leadership practices that have led the chiefs' own subordinates to criticize them.

126

Wheelis offers a theme familiar to much of what has been presented in this study when he writes, "we create ourselves," and goes on to describe the process: "The sequence is suffering, insight, will, action, change. The one who suffers, who wants to change, must bear responsibility all the way" (1973:102).

Wheelis's sequence is not unlike the stages of grieving and recovery outlined by Kubler-Ross (1969). And its resonance is felt by the researcher as he contemplates the recent history of his own agency, suggesting that "death and dying" may be a metaphorically valuable concept even when applied to an organization (Schein, 1985).

The San Diego Police Department has been rocked by what seems to many to be ceaselessly adverse publicity in the recent past, much of it traceable to a violent confrontation that left one officer dead, another wounded and disabled for life, and a civilian "ridealong" also shot and wounded. Two long and highly publicized trials resulted in the acquittal of the young black man who did the shooting. His defense, built on a strategy of self-defense, relied largely upon attacking the attitudes and behavior of the two white officers who stopped him as a possible gang member. Charges of racism and brutality, coupled with allegations of insensitivity on the part of police administrators, were made frequently during the trials. Editorials and community surveys made clear that public confidence in the organization had slipped badly in some quarters—even an erosion of support traditionally found in white, middle-class communities (Decision Research, 1987).

Further, some officers turned their pain and anger toward the department, accusing administrators of jeopardizing their safety through policies perceived as too accommodating to community critics. The department was hurt badly, although it has moved, by all indications, to restore a large measure of public and employee confidence (largely through a commitment

127

to the vision described earlier, the elements of which have been forged into a half-million-dollar in-service training program for all personnel, as well as the work of an 85-member officer safety task force).

It might be said that, given roughly a 10-year prior history of generally excellent relations with the community, the media, and its own employees, the organization witnessed the "death" of its reputation during this period of intense criticism. Certainly, its collective psyche was wounded, and many experienced a loss of pride. When an organization experiences such deep pain and loss, it is perhaps necessary to examine whether the professional *family* has taken the time to process the experience, to mourn the loss, and to rebuild the pride.

Whether the significant change contemplated is on a personal level or an organizational level, a *human* process is being contemplated. Wheelis's prescription bears repeating: "The sequence is suffering, insight, will, action, change. The one who suffers, who wants to change, must bear responsibility all the way."

The Role of Police Executive Management

Kouzes and Posner answer their own question "What is the difference between leaders and managers?" with "leaders bring out the best in us. They get us to achieve even more than we originally believed possible ourselves" (1987:242). The writers go on in increasingly effusive terms about the role and the importance of organizational leadership but say little about organizational management. As did Peters (1984) and many others, what they do have to say about it is not particularly complimentary.

The Place of Executive Management

The popular tendency to denigrate the managerial side of organizational life is most unfortunate. Definitions and distinctions between executive leadership and executive management are given considerable attention in Chapter Two, but important to observe here is that big-city policing in the United States cannot afford to be underled *or* to be ineffectively managed. "Running" a big police bureaucracy requires a thorough understanding of the managerial process and consummate technical skills. From planning to financing and budgeting, and to controlling key processes and employee behavior, effective management of the police agency is of pivotal importance to its success.

Managerial Qualities

In one respect the role of executive management can be neatly summarized as *to know* and *to control*. The police executive manager, must be, as is the leader, thoroughly informed, knowledgeable, and wise about the organization's vision; its history and traditions; its policies, procedures, and practices; and its structural and cultural characteristics and dynamics. Executive managers must also be well educated in the managerial process. They must understand the theory and method of all aspects of *running* a complex political bureaucracy. Further, the executive manager needs to possess most if not all of those qualities associated with the leadership function. Honesty, integrity, toughness, tolerance, interpersonal competence, and credible character are all essential to the success of the big-city police executive manager.

A favorite topic of discussion in academic and leadership development courses seems to center on whether one can be an effective leader without being an effective manager or vice versa. An intuitive response to the question, based on the researcher's experience with the PLPS and within the law enforcement field, is that the police executive must be at least minimally qualified in both disciplines to be successful. However, it is also argued that while the police chief (leader) might not have to be quite as analytical or quite as familiar with the field's technological advances, for example, the assistant chief (manager) must be fully competent in those areas. Still, it is difficult to conceive of either leadership or management being exercised effectively by someone who cannot balance a spreadsheet or understand the interlocking nature of system elements in an organization.

In the next chapter, a model of big-city police executive leadership and executive management is presented. It will be argued that any organization that reveres the one at the expense of the other is not only theoretically asymmetrical in its orientation, it is by definition ineffective or inefficient or both. Further, the neglect of either the executive leadership function or the executive management function serves to ensure deep-seated and widespread antagonisms, dissatisfaction, and alienation both within the ranks and between the police department and the community. At its worst, it could get somebody killed.

Chapter Five

NEW GUIDELINES FOR POLICE EXECUTIVE LEADERSHIP

Presented in this chapter is an introduction to a new way of thinking about police executive leadership and executive management. For at least a few police chiefs, it will look familiar (although it is doubtful that they have seen it presented in this fashion); indeed, some will argue that "we're already doing that." An analysis of the results of the PLPS suggests otherwise.

The presentation of the new model is preceded by a discussion of another model, one that the researcher developed (borrowing liberally from Weisbord's [1976] design) and has been using in team building and other organization development interventions in law enforcement and other governmental organizations. This "model of a healthy organization" is introduced here for the same reason it is used in organizational consulting, namely, to make clear that (1) certain interrelated elements or conditions of an organization must be present for that organization to function effectively and to the satisfaction of both service providers and service recipients; (2) problems that are attributed, frequently in emotional terms, to individuals or to "personalities" can usually be traced to structural origins; and (3) competency in both the leadership functions and the management functions must be demonstrated to develop and sustain a healthy organization.

One suggestion, implicit in the model, is that before concluding that individuals are responsible for organizational problems of effectiveness, efficiency, or workplace morale, the leader or manager should examine carefully the structural elements of the work. Often, as noted, the explanation will be rooted in such elements. This is not, however, meant to excuse inappropriate or unacceptable behavior; individuals must always be held accountable for their performance and their conduct.

Toward a New Model

As exhibited in *Figure 5-1*, the model of a healthy organization has seven components that are brought together by the functions of executive leadership and executive management. Also illustrated is the interdependent nature of the organization's relationship with its external environment.

Figure 5-1
Model of a Healthy Organization

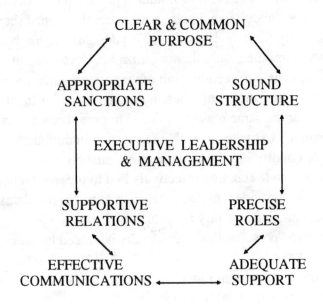

CLEAR & COMMON
PURPOSE

APPROPRIATE
SANCTIONS

SOUND
STRUCTURE

EXECUTIVE LEADERSHIP
& MANAGEMENT

SUPPORTIVE
RELATIONS

PRECISE
ROLES

EFFECTIVE
COMMUNICATIONS

ADEQUATE
SUPPORT

EXTERNAL ENVIRONMENT

Applying this model to the field of big-city policing and, more particularly, to the disciplines of executive leadership and executive management, several things are worth noting about each of its elements, including connections between model elements and responses to the PLPS. In that discussion, the distinctions drawn between the executive leadership function and the executive management function in big-city police departments will become more concrete.

Clear and Common Purpose

Principally a leadership function, this element of the model relates to Item 81 of the PLPS (inspires throughout the organization a shared vision of the future). As noted, there is a very large and highly statistically significant gap between the chiefs' belief in this responsibility and their willingness or ability to fulfill it. Certainly, few things are more important to the police chief than making clear what the organization stands for, what it is here to do, and where the leader wants to lead it in the months and years ahead.

Posited here and borne out by the results of the PLPS, America's big-city police chiefs, with some exceptions, are office-bound managers of their organizations. That reality, it is argued, prevents the chiefs from performing the full range of *leadership* responsibilities so desperately needed by the police organization and the community. Caught up in the day-to-day crush of bureaucratic work and forced to handle the "fire-fighting," damage-controlling duties produced by the exigencies of policing on the streets or politics in the office, the chief executive is understandably not invested in the kind of work that is necessary to crystallize, articulate, and inspire sustained support for a shared vision of the future.

As Block (1987:6) points out in his discussion of organizational life in the private sector,

133

> Most organizations were begun by some-
> one who was willing to bet the farm, but as
> an organization grows and succeeds, it also
> creates the conditions for its own destruc-
> tion. The need for bigness, economy of
> scale, coordination and structure all work
> against the spirit of risk and responsibility
> that breathed life into the firm in the first
> place.

One might wonder if that combination of purposeful and
powerful leadership is inconspicuous in big-city policing because of the nature of the function. In addition to the image-
tarnishing beatings that many police departments take in the
press—sometimes deservedly, sometimes not—a certain underlying reality of the work itself can summon even the deeply
submerged cynicism of the most positive police leaders. That
reality is this: the police agency is not likely to go out of business. "Business as usual," however moribund the usual may
seem, may have become acceptable to practitioners and observers alike because of this truth.

All police departments need leadership that guides and ex-
cites people toward desired social ends, but this is especially
true of those agencies whose personnel have no conception of
their purpose except to arrest "assholes" and answer radio
calls. The community deserves better, and so do the cops.

Sound Structure

To the question of whether America's big-city policing is organized efficiently to get the job done, the answer is a categori-
cal no. The police paramilitary bureaucracy with its layers of
supervisors and managers and functional specialists is simply
too big, too cumbersome, and too unwieldy to serve the purpose of a reasoned and responsible police practice. Evidence
of this reality abounds in the PLPS. Chiefs are shielded from

134

information they must have to appreciate and to meet the needs of their employees.

Similarly, the cop on the beat too frequently gets his or her information about department policies and major events from the media. Team spirit and teamwork are exceedingly difficult to achieve because of the interdependent nature of units that are psychologically if not physically removed from one another, the product of organizational structure. An unhealthy in-group solidarity, often taking the form of cliques or "camps," is fostered by that same structure. Communication, to be addressed later, is stifled, distorted, or otherwise rendered useless or harmful because of these structural problems.

The steep hierarchical nature of the paramilitary bureaucracy is in desperate need of an overhaul. It is at once dysfunctional and exorbitantly expensive. But it is also remarkably resistant to change. Apart from being comfortable with it, many police leaders, it is suggested, are fearful of the labor relations consequences of tampering with it. Civil service traditions, upwardly mobile aspirations of employees, and a variety of other obstacles to reform are quite real and quite tenaciously protected. Big-city chief executives who decide to tackle the challenge of restructuring their police departments have taken on a huge and perilous task. The motives—to make the organization more effective, more efficient, more responsive to the community, even safer and more satisfying to the practitioners—are not likely to be appreciated by most employees, who may see only the denial of promotional opportunity.

And yet, structural reform of American law enforcement is overdue. An invention of the two earlier waves of reform (Fogelson, 1977), the steep chain-of-command needs to be flattened, and the trend toward increased specialization halted, if not reversed. This is a challenge both to the executive leader and to the executive manager. Taking the unpopular stand

135

belongs to the leader. It is to the executive manager and his or her technical expertise that the leader turns for logistical support; it is to the employees, supervisors, and other managers of the organization that the leader turns for input on decisions that will have such a major impact on their lives.

Precise Roles

For people to function effectively in an organization, especially one as rank-heavy and as highly specialized as the police bureaucracy, it is essential that all roles be defined as precisely as possible. As will be made clear later, this is particularly true of the top two positions of the police agency, where the first intraorganizational division between the functions of leadership and management is drawn. But the principle applies equally throughout the organization. Blurred lines of distinction between roles produce confusion and resentment over responsibility and authority for decisions, duties, and privileges. They also have a way of explaining why important work often does not get done well or at all.

In a conversation with Morris Spier (1988), organizational psychologist and professor at United States International University, he spoke of a colleague who had attempted to get him to appreciate how much work she had to do. "I don't think you understand; there's a lot of work to do," she told him. Spier's prescriptive response was "[m]aybe if you look at all that work you'll find a job in there somewhere."

Warren Bennis, cited in Kouzes and Posner (1987:47), after having concluded at about four in the morning that he either "can't manage" or that the University of Cincinnati is unmanageable, made a discovery:

> My discovery was this: I had become the
> victim of a vast, amorphous, unwitting, un-
> conscious conspiracy to prevent me from
> doing anything whatever to change the

136

university's status quo....This discovery...had led to what might be called
Bennis's First Law of Academic Pseudo-
dynamics, to wit: *Routine work drives out
nonroutine work,* or how to smother to
death all creative planning, *all fundamental change in the university—or any
institution.* (Emphasis added.)

Since fundamental change is precisely what is being advanced as a result of this research, it is imperative that the
police chief executive be free to engage in Bennis's "creative
planning."

Unfortunately, PLPS results make unavoidable the conclusion that big-city police chiefs are "too busy" to lead. They
are desk-bound, paper-bound managers. They must transform
themselves into leaders, and perhaps the first place to begin is
by examining how and where they spend their days. It is anticipated that an honest and thoughtful examination would
produce "a job in there somewhere," the job of police leader.
And not that of police manager.

Adequate Support

Safe and successful police work in big cities relies heavily
on at least adequate organizational support. In a world where
bullets travel at a speed of just under 1,000 feet a second, it is
essential that America's police be supported in basic ways.
Every reasonable precaution must be taken to demonstrate
both substantively and symbolically that the safety of the work
force is internal priority one. Personnel selection, education
and training, firepower and other equipment, policies, procedures, and organizational discipline—all must point to the
leader's commitment to reduce the physical risks associated
with big-city police work.

Other forms of support are needed. All employees, regardless of rank or assignment or status, are entitled to a healthy

and comfortable work environment; to a fair and equitable system of compensation, rewards, and sanctions; to education and training; and to the type and quality of information they need to get the job done. They are also, argued in the strongest possible terms, entitled to competent leadership and competent management. Leaders set the tone and the overall priorities; managers see to it that all employees receive at least adequate[*] support.

Effective Communication

This researcher has developed his own definition of effective communication: *a timely and satisfying exchange of relevant, mutually understood information.* It is impossible to imagine an organization's people working effectively and efficiently in the absence of good communication. In police work, detectives or investigators must communicate with patrol officers; nonsworn analysts and others must communicate with both; most employees must communicate with the public; and the executive must communicate with everyone, including his or her bosses in city hall.

Just as the executive must structure expectations (Bass, 1985), so too must he or she structure patterns of organizational communication. Certainly, the manager should be expected

---

[*]While it may seem incongruous to use the term "adequate" in a *model* organization, the wording is purposeful. It notes that public sector employment is likely never to be accorded the kind of financial resources one finds in private enterprise. So, use of the term is intended to suggest to police leaders and managers that their responsibility is to do everything within their power to make sure there is at least enough support. Further, it is also suggested that executives ensure an equitable distribution of suffering if there are insufficient resources to meet all needs amply. This means telling the truth about organizational priorities (e.g., "Yes, we are saying that child abuse investigations are more important than burglary investigation"), and being sensitive to the symbolic meaning when deciding who gets the new car, the next office, the bigger computer.

actually to establish (or, more appropriately, oversee establishment of) the *vehicles* and *networks* of organizational communication; if area stations must communicate with headquarters, if supervisors need to discuss among themselves criteria for employee performance evaluation, if the chief needs to reach the rank and file on a regular basis, how will this be made to happen? This question is properly asked of the manager. But the police chief executive must insist that such vehicles and networks of communication be established and that they be used.

If all personnel of the big-city police agency are to be properly aligned in pursuit of a common purpose or vision, then they must be reasonably *in formation*. The timely and satisfying exchange of relevant, mutually understood information helps to produce this kind of organizational alignment.

On another front, the chief executive who wants to build a high degree of organizational trust might want to consider how much of what kind of information is currently being classified, formally or informally, as "confidential." Sharing widely (with due discretion) "nice to know" as well as "need to know" information is a fine way of developing greater trust in an organization. It also sets in motion the fundamental rule of reciprocity (Cialdini, 1985), which means that the police chiefs are much more likely to get the kind of information they need to be powerful leaders.

The executive's style of interpersonal communication needs careful consideration. The well-intentioned chief who wants, for example, to curtail the use of excessive force by his or her officers might assemble the management team and announce, "I don't ever want to hear of another case of excessive force." A chief who has established a reputation for openness and a demonstrable distaste for the practice of "killing the messenger" might be able to get away with that diction. But even the modestly intimidating or retaliatory style of some

139

executives will help to ensure that the chief will *not* hear of instances of excessive force. Often, what the police chief does not want to hear is what he or she most needs to hear.

Given their "culture-embedding, culture-managing" function (Schein, 1985), police chiefs have to be very careful about such seemingly innocuous displays as a raised eyebrow, a frown, an offhand comment, or an innocent question. Some subordinates are highly susceptible to perceived pressures, however subtle, from their bosses and will draw meaning from a meaningless gesture.

Related to the matter of how the chiefs present their expectations is the question of when they do so. Frequently, in the researcher's experience, chief executives assemble their staffs to ask for input on organizational policies or issues, then promptly offer their own opinion. (This observation is supported by responses to Item 15 of the PLPS; the chiefs purport not to value the idea of police executives running the agency meetings they attend, but the behavior of most, according to a highly significant PLPS finding, says otherwise.) Spontaneity and authenticity are often the victims of this preemptive strike by the boss. Powerful leaders must know what their followers think and feel about organizational issues; indeed, this knowledge is a fundamental source of the leader's power. The prescription then is for police leaders to do what is necessary and reasonable to gain the honest opinions of their followers. That begins with listening to them.

Supportive Relations

One especially important expectation for the leader to structure is that of organizational harmony and support for one another. The work is too important, too sensitive, and too dangerous to allow individuals to indulge in their "personality conflicts." The chief executive, knowing that petty bickering or other interpersonal feuds are inevitable from time to time,

140

must nonetheless set and enforce an expectation that all employees from the top down treat one another as mature, respected adults. Police work as an occupation has more than its share of irresponsible or delinquent behavior (Wambaugh, 1970, 1972). A reasonable question for the chief to explore is why. Is there something in the way the officers are being treated that might suggest an explanation? Returning to an earlier theme, one finds that the way the work of officers is structured will have a powerful effect on their behavior. If they are treated by their bosses as criminals or dependent children, it is simply not reasonable to expect them to act as responsible professionals.

There is an adage, its source lost to the researcher, that the *minimum expected becomes the maximum achieved*—whether one views it as a cynical commentary on human potential or on organized social life. If relevant at all, that message must be heeded. Expecting nothing less than fully competent performance in all areas from all employees at all times is the first expectation the boss should articulate.

It is time to make interpersonal competence at all levels of police work—in the offices and on the streets—a condition of employment.

Appropriate Sanctions

This element of the model of a healthy organization is, like the others, fairly straightforward. Those in the organization who are meeting or exceeding its standards deserve to be recognized for their performance; those whose performance or conduct falls shy of the standards need to be so informed and their work or behavior improved. Of course, the organization's systems of performance evaluation and discipline must be fair and equitable, and the standards on which they are based must be reasonable, job-related, and nondiscriminatory.

Police chiefs were given low marks by the survey for not recognizing excellence or heroism in their employees' performance, at least not to the degree that the chiefs themselves believe is appropriate. That is particularly unfortunate for two reasons: (1) a tremendous amount of such work is being performed by America's street cops and other employees, frequently under extremely adverse conditions, and (2), as a matter of principle, when members of the professional family do exemplary work, they deserve to be recognized for it.

Some police organizations have developed innovative ways to reward their employees for exceptional contributions. The San Diego Police Department, for example, authorizes its commanding officers to award an employee up to three days off with pay under its program of "discretionary leave." In addition to calligraphy-on-parchment commendations and other tangible forms of recognition, most police officers would also appreciate, more than their bosses might imagine, a simple "well done," or a pat on the back. If employee recognition is as important as the chiefs maintain, they must move to structure the expectation that supervisors and managers look to "catch people doing things right" (Peters, 1984). And they must take the seconds necessary to do the same with their immediate subordinates, something the researcher suspects is rarely done.

Generally, as reflected in the PLPS, America's big-city police chiefs are seen as effective agents of control, which is to suggest that they believe in and practice organizational accountability. This observation needs to be evaluated critically. While the PLPS was not designed to provide evidence to that effect, many big-city police departments make little or no distinction between the honest mistakes and the performance problems of their employees, on the one hand, and instances of willful misconduct on the other. There is a large difference, beginning with the motive base, and while it may occasionally be difficult to distinguish between the two, it must be done.

To punish an employee (reprimands, suspensions without pay, punitive transfers) who is working hard and trying to get the job done but who makes an honest mistake is to invite disrespect for the system—and for the police chief, who is generally viewed as responsible for the system.

On the other hand, instances of willful misconduct are not infrequent in police work (Geller, 1985; Stamper, 1977), and this behavior is occasionally overlooked, sometimes because of the popularity of the officer, threatened actions by the union or employee association, or the "hassle" of an overly complicated and inherently adversarial discipline system. Willful misconduct is sometimes ignored because of the politics of the situation; fearing civil liability, or having committed itself to a public defense of the officer's actions, the police agency may opt to "overlook" the employee's transgressions. Those are explanations, but they are not excuses. Policing requires for its credibility, both within the organization and in its relationship with the public, full accountability, no matter what the cost.

This does not suggest that it is unnecessary or unimportant to consider all ramifications of proposed disciplinary actions; on the contrary, the chief executive who does not have legal advice, often stationed within the headquarters building, is rare.[*] Consultations with other officials are also often necessary. And "strategic openness" is essential for any public official. But, in the end, the chief's commitment to truth must extend to all quarters and all circumstances. The leader's integrity is most authentically tested not during calm moments, but during crises.

---

[*]And for good reason, given the increasingly litigious nature of the administration of police discipline.

The External Environment

Police in America belong to the public. They are the "people's police." It is easy to forget such a basic premise when one is caught up in the everyday detail, machinations, and office politics associated with life in the bureaucracy. But it is essential that the police chief executive structure an expectation of *service* to the community. This service orientation needs to be felt at a visceral level by all employees throughout the organization. Even those who do not interact directly with the public, serve the public. They do so through service to others in the agency, and they need to be made to feel that they are an important part of this valuable work.

It is in the nature of big-city police work that a multitude of people outside the agency will want to influence organizational policies, priorities, and practices—state legislators, formal and informal community leaders, citizens-at-large, employee associations, other actors of the criminal justice system, the media, the chief's spouse and children, and families of police officers. That is how it should be in a pluralistic, democratic system of government. Police chiefs need to be open and listen carefully to the needs and fears and concerns of those who would seek to influence police practices. Working collaboratively with disparate groups is not easy, but for the successful police chief it is imperative.

So too is it necessary that the chief executive be a powerful source of influence at all levels of the organization and throughout the community. Policing is too important to be left to amateurs. The police chief executive must behave as—and establish the reputation of—the reigning expert, the community's premier professional on police matters. Legislation, budgets, impressions, and images must be influenced if policing is to achieve the level of respect it deserves and that its leaders have been working so hard to achieve.

Executive Leadership and Executive Management

At the heart of the model of a healthy organization are the functions—the separate functions—of executive leadership and executive management. The competent performance of each is a requisite to organizational effectiveness, efficiency, and job satisfaction. Posited below is a concept calling for a distinct division of labor between American police chiefs and their immediate assistants, between the interdependent and complementary functions of executive leadership and executive management.

A Paradigm Shift

Given the results of this research, police leadership is what chiefs are forced to do in their spare time. Purposeful and powerful police executive leadership is a full-time job. So too is responsible and accountable police executive management. American big-city police chiefs, according to the results of the PLPS, are trying to do both full-time jobs. And their performance in each reflects the unfortunate consequences, according to their assistants. The chiefs place a very high value on virtually all of the leadership variables of the PLPS, but their actual behavior falls short of those values. Conversely, they place a comparatively low value on their personal involvement in the managerial work of the organization, but their actual behavior suggests that they play a direct and active role in managing their agencies.

Because most big-city chiefs in the United States are struggling to be both full-time leaders and full-time managers, and because they *cannot* do both, each function suffers. Corporate America has understood for years the necessity of a division of labor at the top of the organization. The chief executive officer handles the leadership functions; the chief operating officer conducts the management process.

It is time for a change, a fundamental paradigm shift.
Police chiefs of America's big cities must become full-time
leaders of their agencies. They can no longer afford to let the
nature of the modern paramilitary police bureaucracy take its
own course. They must devote their attention and their ener-
gies to *structuring expectations* (Bass, 1985) and *embedding
and managing organizational culture* (Schein, 1985). As
Schein observes, "there is a possibility—underemphasized in
leadership research—that the *only thing of real importance
that leaders do is to create and manage culture...*" (1985:2).
Schein calls this the "unique talent" of leaders and goes on to
suggest that the only way to demystify leadership and to make
it a thing of power and purpose is to separate it from
management.

Scope of Change

The scope of change called for here is not modest. It calls
for police chiefs to get out of the office, abandoning Skousen's
(1977) admonition that they "run a hot desk," that they show
the world how "busy" they are. It envisions America's big-
city police chiefs fully and influentially engaged—as their
agencies' "living emblem" (Peters, 1984)—both with the community they have been appointed to serve and with their own
employees, whose work shapes the reputation of the organization. And it means turning over the managerial reins to a
trusted "second in command."

It will not be easy. The police chiefs rather soundly rejected
the idea in their response to Item 17 (delegates day-to-day responsibility for management of the agency to a trusted subordinate).[*]

---

*It is possible, perhaps likely, that the chief executives view the
terms "management" and "leadership" synonymously, in which case it is
understandable that they should be reluctant to delegate such responsibility. Nonetheless, their involvement in other managerial functions
makes quite clear the chiefs' behavioral orientation. They spend a great
deal of time managing their agencies.

146

Other evidence of their unwillingness or inability to make organizational leadership their full-time occupation is their tendency to run the meetings they attend (Item 15); to have ready answers to technical questions (Item 84); to be able to answer immediately operational questions from their bosses (Item 28); and, perhaps most convincingly, to spend as much time as possible in the office, attending to the business of the agency (Item 20). This pattern of behavior, it is argued, is deeply rooted in structural causation. It has little to do with the "personalities" or, for that matter, the preferences of the chiefs.

The New Model

Figure 5-2 presents the two functions of police administration: executive leadership and executive management. It not only reflects the paradigm shift but also suggests where both the chief executive and the assistant chief should spend the greatest percentage of their time.

It is important to point out that executive leadership and executive management are presented as two separate and clearly distinguishable dimensions of big-city police administration. Put differently, those two positions represent two different jobs altogether. As practiced today in many law enforcement agencies, the two functions are virtually indistinguishable. The chief and the assistant handle the same paperwork and participate, in roughly equal amounts of time, in common decision-making and problem-solving activities; with the exception of most ceremonial and political activities (the principal domain of the chief executive), their roles are, by and large, interchangeable.

Figure 5-2

**Executive Leadership and Executive Management:
The Two Functions of Police Administration**

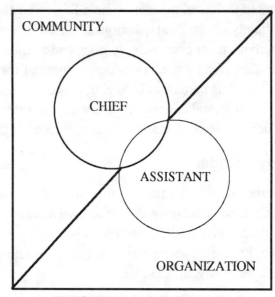

As seen in *Figure 5-2,* while a clear distinction is drawn between executive leadership and executive management, the
two functions must also overlap in certain respects. For example, it is essential that the police chief executive (leader) be
thoroughly familiar with critical dimensions of the work of the
assistant chief (manager). Likewise, it is imperative that the
manager be fully informed of the organization's vision and
demonstrate leadership qualities even as he or she generally
does not engage in the function. Further, the assistant chief is
frequently called upon to act in lieu of the chief executive
when the police chief is unavailable.

A few additional comments on that middle ground of overlapping responsibilities are in order. First, this model as all
other theoretical models is intended to serve as a guidepost to
actual practices. Although it is derived from data produced by

America's big-city police chiefs and their assistants, those officials were responding to questions put to them by an outside party, one who has little if any appreciation of the details of their organizational arrangements and pressures.

Second, because of historical and other differences that exist from one agency to the next (thereby rendering each police department unique), it would be both impossible and presumptuous to list specific tasks, duties, and responsibilities that ought to fall to the chief and those that should be handled by the assistant.

Third, for the foregoing reasons, whether it is dictated by the chief (not recommended) or negotiated between the chief and the assistant (highly recommended), the two sets of responsibilities ought to overlap in ways that make sense operationally. For example, budgeting might be seen as the responsibility of the assistant chief, but the chief executive would probably want to establish parameters and set up some mechanism for regular briefings on budget status. Fourth, if the area of overlapping responsibilities becomes too great or if any shared responsibilities are not carefully articulated as such, the intended outcome, namely, an *operational* distinction between executive leadership and executive management, will not be realized.

Finally, one needs to understand that, while this model most certainly calls for the assistant to "run" the organization, in the sense of *managing* its day-to-day operations, that does not mean the assistant functions autonomously. Everything the assistant chief does—or does not do—must be seen by the organization as aligned with the thinking, the vision, and the philosophy of the chief of police. The two parties must be perceived by the community and by agency personnel as working in tandem, complementing each other and carrying out a deliberate, structured division of labor intended to bring strength to both major functions of police administration.

Dimensions of Big-City Police Executive Leadership and Executive Management

To understand how this model might work in practice, attention is turned to the nine factors that were found to underlie the PLPS—four leadership factors and five management factors—which are now presented as the key *dimensions* of big-city police executive leadership and executive management. Implicit in those dimensions is the message that police executive leaders and police executive managers have different jobs to do. Their work should be of two distinctly different characters, and they should be spending their days differently.

Leadership Dimension No. 1: Modeling Expected Behavior

There are 23 PLPS items contained within this dimension. A strong theme that emerges centers on the leader as an activist, as a doer, and as one who inspires a shared vision of the future and whose behavior communicates integrity and credibility. Leaders establish expectations for—and model—the kind of behavior that is expected from all employees. This dimension also has a strong developmental nature, reflecting a belief that one of the most valuable legacies of a leader is to be replaced by someone better when it is time to depart. On the premise that the world of police executive leadership gets tougher and not easier with the passage of time, it is imperative that today's leaders work to be replaced by successors who are more knowledgeable, more skillful, and at least as dedicated as they. This can happen if the incumbent leader makes a conscious decision, and sees that programs are created, to promote the personal growth and professional development of his or her subordinates.

150

Leadership Dimension No. 2: Exhibiting Interest and Concern

The police chief who embraces this value lets people know they are important. He or she visits hospitalized members, meets with families of slain or injured officers, and takes time to express concern and support. He or she also wears the agency's uniform from time to time, a gesture that indicates the chief's desire to remain in touch with the work and with the people who do that work. Because subordinates tend to pay attention to what the boss attends to, those leaders who develop a habit of caring communicate an important message about how they want other managers and supervisors to behave.

Leadership Dimension No. 3: Serving the Community

The police chief executive never loses sight of the purpose of the organization: to protect and to serve the community. In order to understand community needs, police chiefs must spend a large percentage of their time attending neighborhood meetings; inviting and listening to citizen input on agency priorities and practices; and, in a strategy that does "double duty," riding or walking along with patrol officers and investigators to stay in touch with the community. This last strategy deserves special attention. The PLPS indicates that the chiefs' time with the community is "favored" over time spent in the organization. In the view of police executive leadership presented here, the chiefs while spending time in the community are usually in the company of other police personnel (e.g., the area captain, the beat officer). By this means, the chiefs seize an important opportunity to model the kind of behavior toward the community that is expected of all personnel. This strategy in particular is posited as an exceptionally powerful approach to structuring organizational expectations.

Leadership Dimension No. 4: Valuing Openness and Diversity

The effective police chief is one who not only tolerates but appreciates questioning and criticism of agency policies and practices. If "information is power," and it clearly is at least one important source of power, the chiefs who are open to and respectful of others' opinions position themselves to gain valuable information and to strengthen their base of executive power. For many, that requires an appreciation of the distinction between Thompson's concepts of "personal face" and "professional face" (Task Force on Human Relations Training, 1986). Thompson argues that cops, including the agency's top cop, are "not paid to express their personal opinions." He does not maintain that police officers are not entitled to personal views on the issues they confront, merely that as public servants they have a responsibility to know and to control their personal biases. The police chief who can do that stands to gain much. Having listened respectfully and heard accurately what others are saying, he or she is far more qualified to present and, if necessary, defend agency positions.

Management Dimension No. 1: Setting Standards

Whether in the area of investigators' case cancellations, the use of agency overtime, receiving and sending correspondence, or in a variety of other examples including overall agency performance, the day-to-day work of a complex organization requires standards. In an important sense, a standard answers the question "How good is good enough?" The assistant chief, under general guidance from the police chief, must see to it that such standards are set and communicated to all involved.

As noted earlier, those standards must be reasonable, job-related, and nondiscriminatory. They must also conform to the agency's vision. And because many of them will require financing, the assistant chief must ensure that the agency's standards (and the priorities formed by them) are consistent with the department's financial capacity to support them.

Management Dimension No. 2: Keeping Promises

It is particularly in this dimension that the "hands-on" nature of effective management is located. The idea is simple: the assistant chief must know, understand, and control—mostly through subordinate managers—the process of *managing promises*. If the agency's vision, for example, speaks of inspired performance on the streets, the manager must be assured that the department's supervisory practices are sound, its performance evaluation and disciplinary systems working as intended, and its programs of education and training timely and relevant. Likewise for other systems: the receipt and handling of citizen complaints, vehicle fleet and other equipment maintenance, radio and other communications systems, computer programs, and all other forms of organizational support for effective policing on the streets.

Management Dimension No. 3: Maintaining Technical Competence

While unlikely that the number-two person in the organization will be involved intimately in the detail work of his or her responsibilities, it is essential that the assistant chief develop and maintain a high-degree of technical expertise. On all fronts, the work has become more technically and more technologically sophisticated. The assistant must be familiar with the latest advances in methods of planning, budgeting, organizing, monitoring, and controlling. For large, decentralized police agencies, it is imperative that the assistants' knowledge and understanding of communication links (telecommunications and other technologies) be sufficient to make them conversant in the field.

Management Dimension No. 4: Thinking and Behaving Rationally

Decision making in a large bureaucracy relies for its effectiveness on the collection and analysis of a wide range of information. Chief executives, under this model, turn to their assistant chiefs for accurate, timely, and thoroughly analyzed information. From revenue and spending forecasts to crime pattern analysis to shifts in community demographic characteristics and called-for service demands, the organization must have meaningful information upon which to base its decisions. That is especially true for the appropriation, allocation, and distribution of increasingly expensive resources. To this end, assistant chiefs need to possess solid analytical skills and an analytical temperament. Events in policing tend to produce highly emotional reactions. The assistants cannot be immune to these emotions, including their own. But, to be of greatest service to both the organization and the community, the assistant should strive to be as logical, dispassionate, and analytical as possible.

Management Dimension No. 5: Demonstrating Fiscal Responsibility

Here the case is made that the assistant chief should be seen as *the* budget director of the organization. This function is crucial to the success both of the day-to-day operations of the organization and to the realization of its vision. As such, it should be elevated to the status of the preeminent management function, and the assistant chief should accept personal responsibility for its success.

Planning, especially long-range planning, is closely linked to the budgeting process. Yet support for the function is notoriously weak in many police agencies (in part because of the understandable tendency of many inside and outside the organization to view policing in reactive rather than creative or proactive terms; such is the nature of the traditional practice of "reacting" to crimes and "responding" to radio calls). Planning does not receive the attention it deserves.

Similarly, the budgeting process itself tends to be viewed by many as a frustrating seasonal exercise in which lower level supervisors submit requests knowing that they will never receive feedback and only rarely the items they requested. The assistant chief can and should make the budgeting-planning process a rational and continuous year-round activity, one that all members of the organization can understand and perhaps even influence.

Other Levels of Police Leadership and Management

This study has examined *executive* leadership and management. As such, it has concentrated its attention on the roles of the top two positions in the police organization, the chief and the assistant chief. It is important to note, however, that changes as significant as those contemplated here are bound to have profound effects on the work of people at levels lower than the executive suite. Further, the reactions of middle managers and first-line supervisors, for example, would surely set in motion structural changes of their own, only a few of which might be anticipated. For this reason alone, it is essential that any shifts in the responsibilities of the chief and the assistant chief be carefully deliberated. Two suggestions are offered.

Dividing Labor Between Chief and Assistant

The first suggestion is as basic as it is important: the chief and the assistant chief, having committed themselves to making one the leader of the organization and the other its manager, should spend as much time as necessary thinking about which tasks and duties belong to the one position and

155

which to the other. The decision should be based on the question "Is this particular duty or task a leadership function or is it a managerial function?"

It would be helpful to think in terms of *structuring expectations* and *embedding organizational culture*. If the task considered does not fall into those categories, if it conjures up visions of protracted meetings, computer printouts, time in the office, then it almost certainly does not belong under the chief's name.

The advice and counsel of others would undoubtedly be helpful. And each might want to start a list, keeping it within arm's reach for a certain period of time. When ready, the two should find a place where they will not be interrupted and begin the process of negotiating the placement of each task. Again, a case can be made for an overlapping category in which both the chief and the assistant chief share certain responsibilities.

The result of this division of labor needs to be communicated widely and clearly. That can be done as the culmination of the exercise, or it can signal the beginning of much broader organizational change.

The researcher is committed to the proposition that the model presented in this chapter, while a necessary means of strengthening executive leadership and management, is limited in its potential if its underlying premise is not extended down through the ranks, affecting in the process every supervisor and manager in the agency.

The Leader-Manager Model Extended

If it makes sense to separate the leadership from the management functions at the executive level, would it not also be wise to do so at other levels? The answer, it is argued, is yes—for precisely the same reason posited for the top of the organization, to strengthen both leadership and management.[*]

To illustrate, a police department with seven levels of supervision and management will have (titles vary from one jurisdiction to the next) a chief; one or more assistant chiefs (more than one poses, at least theoretically, a problem that will be addressed momentarily); several deputy chiefs; commanders; captains; lieutenants; and sergeants. That constitutes the chain of command. (It also helps explain why the steep hierarchically arranged police paramilitary bureaucracy produces a substantial amount of "incremental whitewashing," as well as legitimate filtering of information as that information is passed from one level to the next.)

Having already addressed the top two roles in considerable detail, attention is turned to the deputy chief position. Following the agency's top manager in the chain of command, the deputy chief is a leader. As such, he or she should be expected to be "out and about," visible and conspicuous as a leader of a major functional division of the agency. Reporting to the deputy chief are commanders, whose function should be management. If anyone is to be desk-bound or paper-bound in that relationship it should be the commander, in part because

---

*In an empirically unevaluated test of the hypothesis outlined in this section, the researcher employed from 1984 to 1986 the concept of the alternating leader-manager within the ranks of deputy chief through sergeant while in charge of the office of field operations of the San Diego Police Department. This was done with the permission and support of the then-assistant chief, Robert W. Burgreen, to whom much of the credit is owed. Several transfers of personnel have taken place at the deputy chief level since then, and the concept has been unevenly applied since 1986. But it does represent the first step by a major police department in the direction of an agencywide restructuring of the roles of supervisors and managers. It should also be noted that the executive-level division of labor in that organization closely approximates the model, with the chief responsible for overall leadership and the assistant chief in charge of day-to-day operations.

the managerial nature of his or her work serves to free up for leadership activities both the deputy chief *and* the captains who report to the commander. The same applies to the relationship between the captain and the lieutenants, with the lieutenants also handling the managerial side of the work in their relationship with the sergeants.

Perhaps the most important benefit to be realized by restructuring the work along these lines is that the first-line supervisors, the sergeants, will have time to be in the field. Few occupations are in as much need of competent first-line supervision as policing. Much has been made throughout this study of the complexity, the sensitivity, and the danger of contemporary police work. It needs to be guided by strong, professional supervisors who are not only capable but also have been given time to devote the bulk of their efforts to directing and coaching their officers. This is particularly true of police patrol work, where typically the youngest and least mature of the work force toil. Further, as noted previously, fine police work needs to be recognized and poor performance and misconduct need to be corrected. Those most basic supervisory responsibilities are difficult to meet if the sergeant (leader) is in the office doing paperwork that could and should be done by the lieutenant (manager).

The institution of big-city policing must come to the realization that competent leadership and competent management are essential at all levels of the organization.

Potential Barriers

There are many potential obstacles to the adoption or successful implementation of the leader-manager model. With the focus now shifted back to the chief and assistant chief for the remainder of this chapter, several of these barriers are identified.

The Work Ethic

Most big-city police chiefs, having worked their way up through the ranks of their agencies, have established reputations as hard-working individuals. "Work" in police administration is cast typically as spending 10, 12, 14 hours per day in the office, conferring with senior staff members, reviewing staff reports, and conducting planning or budget meetings. To suddenly stop all that and to begin spending time riding along with officers, attending roll call sessions, or visiting with residents in a housing project would be, for some, tantamount to job abandonment.

External Pressures

Even if the chief executive is psychologically prepared for the change, others may not be. If the mayor or the city manager is accustomed to finding the chief in the office, and if the chief is quick with answers to technical or operational questions when asked by significant others, it may be very difficult to make the adjustment to a leadership mode.

Lack of a Trusted Subordinate

It would be interesting to learn how many of the chiefs responded to Item 17 of the PLPS (delegating day-to-day responsibility to a trusted subordinate) believing that they had *no one* to whom they could turn over the managerial reins because of a lack of confidence in their assistants' capabilities or trustworthiness. In any event, a certain barrier to adoption of the model would be the chief's perception that the assistant could not be trusted with the critical responsibility of managing the police organization.

Multiple Assistants

Many big-city police departments have more than one "second in command." While this "obstacle" could be overcome, it would certainly be more difficult to implement the concept under the condition of multiple assistant chiefs.

Fear of Wandering

Tom Peters (1984) tells a story about a group of business people who were listening to one of his speeches. He was telling them about the Hewlitt-Packard program (Peters and Waterman, 1982) in which executives engage in "management by wandering around." One of the executives approached him and, quite emotionally, admitted, "But, Tom, I don't know *how* to wander." The same, presumably, could be said about some big-city police chiefs. As hard as it might be to imagine, given their position and their status, some chiefs would likely find it a struggle to leave the security of their offices and engage the work force or the community in any meaningful fashion. The longer they have been away, the more difficult and painful could be their re-entry.

Bureaucratic Inertia

All systems have a way of resisting change and, for that matter, fighting back when they are asked to do so (Kauffman, 1980). For this reason, and others too numerous to describe here, the leader-manager model can reasonably be expected to be resisted, strenuously by some. In its pure form, the concept calls for sweeping changes in the nature of work performed by at least the top two people of the police agency. Especially if the chief is comfortable with the status quo, it is highly unlikely that this kind of change would be received favorably.

Rejection of the Concept

An understandable reason for not wanting to adopt the leader-manager model is the chief's rejection of its premise or, perhaps, certain aspects of the concept. Similarly, the suggestion of a need for change may be seen as an assumption that the chiefs are not already doing what is being offered here as a major change. As noted earlier, some chiefs—including many whose values and behavior have been found in this research to be inconsistent with each other—are convinced that they are practicing, if not to the letter, the principles implicit in the model.

Responses to Barriers

Should big-city chiefs or those attempting to influence their chiefs see merit in the model and want to proceed with its implementation, several cautions are suggested. The first is to respect those potential barriers identified above. If they do not contain "objective" reasons for failing to proceed, at least they imply legitimate feelings, including fear of and skepticism toward the change. In the spirit of the type of leadership being proposed in this study, people's feelings must be honored. That does not mean that efforts to influence opponents should be abandoned. It simply means that their opposition needs to be heard and understood.

To the chief who decides to implement some version of this model, the following suggestions are offered: (1) move slowly; (2) invite wide participation in the deliberations and planning but do not "pull punches" (if the decision has been made to operationalize a distinction between executive leadership and executive management, needed credibility will be traded for cynicism and, in all likelihood, subversion if the "decision" is presented as negotiable); (3) begin immediately the process of structuring expectations by visiting with people whose support is needed, letting them know that their thoughts and feelings are important, and listening to them; (4) make certain that *all* parties to the decision, including those who are only indirectly involved, are made aware of what will change and how they will be affected (this move is especially important for those who have come to expect a certain pattern of behavior from the chief and assistant chief); (5) once the decision is made, *refuse* to manage, respecting the newly defined jurisdiction of the assistant; and (6) begin immediately and continue ceaselessly the process of executive leadership by becoming visible and conspicuous in the leadership arena—it is where the leader belongs.

Epilogue

This researcher is acquainted with several big-city police chiefs and, through this research, has been "introduced" to many others. The PLPS produced strong evidence that the executive behavior of these chiefs generally does not support their claim to the values they profess. That was not unexpected. Virtually all "self/other" instruments produce similar results. Further, in fairness to them, the chiefs were not asked to describe their behavior; they were asked to express their values. How many of us can claim to practice fully what we preach? Finally, it needs to be said that the job of the big-city police chief is one of the most difficult in the country and, by and large, it is done remarkably well under the circumstances. Whether it is being done as well as it needs to be is subject to debate, but few in the field would argue that it cannot be improved.

One promising avenue to improvement would be the adoption of the model outlined herein. Of particular promise is the prospect of substantially strengthening executive leadership in the future by means of the alternating leader-manager-leader career path. By the time one arrives in the executive office, he or she will have been exposed to something approximating "pure" leadership and "pure" management. Adoption of the model could, arguably, produce chief executives in the future who, while intimately familiar with the crucial functions of the managerial process, can provide truly inspired police leadership.

This researcher's bias should be clear by now: Executive leadership has been "structured out" of police administration. The time has come for a more powerful form of big-city police leadership, one that can make of American policing the kind of respected and respectful institution it struggles to become.

164

GLOSSARY

Brutality

American police officers are empowered to use, in Bittner's (1970) words, "non-negotiably coercive force," including lethal force if necessary. The test is whether the force used is "reasonable," as judged by a "reasonable and prudent" person; the standard varies from state to state. Any force beyond that which is reasonable is treated herein as an act of brutality.

Centrist

A person who occupies the precise middle ground between the pure leader and the pure manager. A synthesis of traits, attitudes, beliefs, values, and behaviors. Essentially splits time between leadership and managerial activities.

Chief executive

That one individual who, within the organizational context, is ultimately responsible for the overall effectiveness, efficiency, and morale of agency personnel, as well as the community-police relationship.

Citizens

Refers to all people with whom the police interact in the community. Includes inhabitants and those who work in, visit, or pass through the city regardless of legal citizenship.

City policing	That range of crime-fighting, traffic, and other services provided by municipal police officers. This study does not address law enforcement by any other level of government, federal, state, or county. While the work of county sheriffs may, in many respects, be functionally identical to that of city police officers, certain responsibilities (administration of a jail or court services, for example) or aspects of agency leadership (elected versus appointed chief executives) either present confounding variables or extend beyond the scope of this study.
Community relations	While "community relations" often refers to a specialized relations unit within the police organization, its use here refers to the overall quality of the relationship between the agency's personnel and the citizens they serve.
Corruption	Any breach of the public trust, including but not limited to, theft, acceptance of bribes, extortion, blackmail, embezzlement, ticket-fixing, or any other unlawful or unethical act committed under color of authority.
Crime fighting	Those acts undertaken by a police agency or a police officer to prevent crime, detect and apprehend criminal offenders, and assist in the prosecution of offenders through investigation, scientific

analysis, reporting, and testimony in court.

Ideology   An individual's conceptualization of the world. As defined by Lauer (1982:182), ideologies are "legitimations of a particular order; they arise out of that order, and they tend to perpetuate it by adorning it with legitimacy."

Leader   Functions as the "living emblem" of the organization. At the polar extreme of the pure manager, the pure leader embodies, or personifies, what the organization stands for, and believes in. He or she is visible and conspicuous in the organization and in the community. Does little or no "hands-on" or detailed work. Only occasionally in the office; usually found in the hallways, offices of others, and in the field. Committed to embedding organizational culture through calculated process of interpersonal relationships; talks directly to as many employees as possible. Encourages openness, risk-taking, use of intuition, and creativity. Strong commitment to personal growth and professional development, both in self and in subordinates. Open to—and actively encourages—questioning and criticism of organizational policies and practices. Very quick to praise others. Known for his or her political acumen. Shares responsibility for leadership. Orientation

167

is in the future. Inspires a common and inspiring vision for the organization.

Leader-manager   Orientation is toward the pure leader functions. More active than the leader in setting, monitoring, and controlling organizational objectives, priorities, and expectations for performance and conduct. Is concerned about meeting management obligations, but usually does so through others, spending most time in the high-profile leadership arena. Time spent with others is somewhat more structured than that of pure leader. Tends to be more specific than the leader in expectations of others, especially subordinates. Encourages initiative, open to change, but less likely than the pure leader to invite risk-taking. More likely than the pure leader to require systematic evaluation of people and programs. Looks to the future, but language is likely to reflect an interest in goals and objectives rather than a "vision."

Leadership   Influencing others to act, and to want to act, in accordance with socially desirable behaviors and toward socially desirable ends. Executive leadership and management refer to the functions of the individuals who perform at the policy-making and highest policy-execution levels of the agency.

Management

The transaction of existing conditions that may or may not be conducive to the creation of a socially desirable future state. Management concentrates on ensuring that the job gets done.

Manager

A controlling manager whose time is spent almost exclusively in his or her office, which serves as the "command center" for the organization. The lion's share of the agency's paper originates from and returns to this office. Personally balances spread sheets, maintains statistics on most organization/managerial processes. Coordination and control are accomplished principally by telephone, computer, and memoranda. Sees himself or herself, and is seen by others, as very analytical and dispassionate. Does a great deal of reading, most of it directly related to indices of organizational effectiveness and efficiency. Rarely seen at work-connected parties or other social events or organizational ceremonies. New ideas are of interest if they are perceived as valuable in controlling the managerial process; intuitive and creative suggestions are often rejected with disdain. Seen by those "in the know" as the one who controls resources and who has answers to most questions about the organization's past. Nonetheless, orientation is in the present, getting the job done today.

Manager-leader

Orientation is toward the pure manager functions, but does get out and about in the organization; relatively little contact with the community. Personally sees to it that key organizational processes (those having to do with budget, safety equipment, management information systems, and the like) are functioning smoothly. Coordinates by going from office to office, seeing to it that loose ends are tied together. Sees himself or herself as a problem solver. Has a more personal style of management than that of the pure manager. Likes to deal in "specifics," to develop with others concrete indices of organizational effectiveness and efficiency. Usually follows—and expects others to follow—the organization's chain of command. Has reputation for holding people accountable. More interested in organization's current image and reputation than its place in the future, but is mindful of future implications of today's decisions.

Officer safety

Emerging as a specialized discipline within policing, "officer safety" refers, in the context of this study, to an end state. Such a state has been achieved when policing has been rendered as safe as it can be. Its significance is such that any effort intended to reform police work is destined to fail if the police practitioner's personal well-

170

being is neglected or in any other way compromised by his or her boss.

Order maintenance   Those police service duties, constituting the largest portion of a patrol officer's time, that have little or only an indirect relationship to crime fighting. Examples include regulating the flow of traffic, mediating family and neighborhood disputes, assisting stranded motorists, searching for lost children, and attempting to regulate human conduct through such strategies as foot patrol and random citizen contacts.

Organizational culture   "A pattern of basic assumptions," according to Schein (1985:9), that are "invented, discovered, or developed by a given group as it learns to cope with its problems of external adaptation and internal integration...." Those basic assumptions are strong enough to show the organization's personnel the "correct way to perceive, think, and feel..." (Schein, 1985:9). Reuss-Ianni (1983) writes of "two cultures" of policing, the culture of the manager and the culture of the cop. Both are pivotal elements of this study.

Organizational structure   Broadly defined to include not only the agency's table of organization but also individual and institutional attitudes, values, policies, procedures, and practices—both past and present. In other

171

	words, virtually any condition that structures organizational behavior.
Paramilitary bureaucracy	An organizational arrangement that borrows heavily from Weberian principles and "scientific management" and is imbued with the trappings, nomenclature, and commitment to rule making and rule enforcement associated with the military model.
Police chief	The chief executive of a city police department. May also be known in some jurisdictions as "colonel," "superintendent," "public safety director" (especially when also responsible for fire fighters, lifeguards, or other safety services personnel), or "commissioner." The police chief executive in this study is appointed, not elected.
Police officer	An individual hired, usually through a civil service selection process, to perform basic police functions in the city. Strictly speaking, the chief executive is almost always a sworn police officer too, that is, he or she has enforcement powers. However, for purposes of this study, "police officer" refers to the cop on the beat, the detective, or other specialist at the entry level. (Also essentially beyond the scope of this study are the police agency's supervisors and middle managers.)

Reform A change in the structure, composition, direction, practices, or other constituent properties of American law enforcement intended to improve both the substance and the image of city policing. This research recognizes the significance and the polemics of the "radical versus reformist" debate but does not engage it.

REFERENCES CITED

Abdel-Halim, Ahmed A. 1983. "Power Equalization, Participative Decision-Making, and Individual Differences." *Human Relations* 36, no. 8, pp. 683-704.

Adams, Ronald J.; McTernan, Thomas M.; and Remsberg, Charles. 1985. *Street Survival: Tactics for Armed Encounters.* Northbrook, Illinois: Calibre Press.

Ad Hoc Task Force on Police Practices. 1979. *Ad Hoc Task Force on Police Practices: Final Report.* San Diego, California: City of San Diego.

Alex, Nicholas. 1969. *Black in Blue: A Study of the Negro Policeman.* New York: Appleton-Century-Crofts.

American Bar Association. 1973. *Standards Relating to the Urban Police Function.* Chicago: American Bar Association.

Anderson, John C., and Reilly, Charles A., III. 1981. "Effects of an Organizational Control System on Managerial Satisfaction and Performance." *Human Relations* 34, no. 6, pp. 491-501.

Andrews, Allen H., Jr. 1985. "Structuring the Political Independence of the Police Chief." In *Police Leadership in America: Crisis and Opportunity.* Edited by William A. Geller. New York: Praeger.

Angell, John. 1973. "Toward an Alternative to the Classic Police Organizational Arrangements: A Democratic Model." In *Issues in Police Patrol: A Book of Readings.* Edited by Thomas J. Sweeney and William Ellingsworth. Washington, D.C.: Police Foundation.

Argyris, Chris, and Schon, Donald A. 1978. *Organizational Learning: A Theory of Action Perspective.* Reading, Massachusetts: Addison-Wesley Publishing.

Balkan, Sheila; Berger, Ronald J.; and Schmidt, Janet. 1980. *Crime and Deviance in America: A Critical Approach.* Belmont, California: Wadsworth Publishing Company.

Barnard, C. I. 1968. *The Functions of An Executive.* 1938 Reprint. Cambridge, Massachusetts: Harvard University.

Bass, Bernard M. 1981. *Stogdill's Handbook of Leadership.* New York: The Free Press.

_____. 1985. *Leadership and Performance Beyond Expectations.* New York: The Free Press.

Bayley, David H., and Mendelsohn, Harold. 1968. *Minorities and the Police: Confrontation in America.* New York: The Free Press.

Bennis, Warren, and Nanus, Burt. 1985. *Leaders: The Strategies For Taking Charge.* New York: Harper and Row.

Berkley, George E. 1969. *The Democratic Policeman.* Boston: Beacon Press.

Bittner, Egon. 1970. *The Functions of the Police in Modern Society.* Chevy Chase, Maryland: National Institute of Mental Health.

Block, Peter. 1987. *The Empowered Manager: Positive Political Skills at Work.* San Francisco: Jossey-Bass Publishers.

Blumberg, Abraham S., and Niederhoffer, Elaine, eds. 1985. *The Ambivalent Force: Perspectives on the Police.* 3d rev. ed. New York: Holt, Rinehart, and Winston.

Bouza, Anthony V. 1985. "Police Unions: Paper Tigers or Roaring Lions?" In *Police Leadership in America: Crisis and Opportunity.* Edited by William A. Geller. New York: Praeger.

Boydstun, John E. 1975. *San Diego Field Interrogation: Final Report.* Washington, D.C.: Police Foundation.

Boydstun, John E., and Sherry, Michael E. 1975. San Diego Community Profile: Final Report. Washington, D.C.: Police Foundation.

Boydstun, John E.; Sherry, Michael; and Moelter, Nicholas. 1977. *San Diego One-Officer/Two-Officer Car Study.* Washington, D.C.: Police Foundation.

Bradford, David L., and Cohen, Allan R. 1984. *Managing for Excellence.* New York: John Wiley and Sons.

Brancato, Gilda, and Polebaum, Elliott E. 1981. *The Rights of Police Officers: An American Civil Liberties Union Handbook.* New York: Avon Books.

Bristow, Allen P. 1975. *You and the Law Enforcement Code of Ethics.* Santa Cruz, California: Davis Publishing Company.

Brown, L. David. 1986. "Power Outside Organizational Paradigms." In *Executive Power: How Executives Influence People and Organizations.* Edited by Srivastva and Associates. San Francisco: Jossey-Bass.

Brown, Lee P. 1985. "Police-Community Power Sharing." In *Police Leadership in America: Crisis and Opportunity*. Edited by William A. Geller. New York: Praeger.

Burleson, Brant R.; Levine, Barbara J.; and Saunter, Wendy. 1984. "Decision-Making Procedure and Decision Quality." *Human Communication Research* 10, no. 4 (Summer), pp. 557-574.

Burns, James MacGregor. 1978. *Leadership*. New York: Harper and Row.

Carte, Gene E., and Carte, Elaine H. 1975. *Police Reform in the United States: The Era of August Vollmer, 1905-1932*. Berkeley, California: University of California Press.

Cartwright, Dorwin, and Zander, Alvin, eds. 1968. *Group Dynamics: Research and Theory*. New York: Harper and Row.

Chevigny, Paul. 1969. *Police Power: Police Abuses in New York City*. New York: Vintage Press.

Cialdini, Robert B. 1985. *Influence: Science and Practice*. Glenview, Illinois: Scott, Foresman and Company.

Citizens Interracial Committee of San Diego County. 1969. "Special Report on *Sunday in the Park: July 13, 1969*." San Diego, California: The Citizens Interracial Committee of San Diego County, Inc.

Clark, Ramsey. 1970. *Crime in America*. New York: Simon and Schuster.

Commission on Peace Officer Standards and Training. 1986. *POST Administrative Manual*. Sacramento, California: State of California.

Cooper, Lynn, et al. 1975. *The Iron Fist and the Velvet Glove: An Analysis of the U.S. Police.* Berkeley, California: Center for Research on Criminal Justice.

Cordery, John L., and Wall, Toby D. 1985. "Work Design and Supervisory Practice: A Model." *Human Relations* 38, no. 5, pp. 425-441.

Cornish, Edward, ed. 1977. *The Study of the Future: An Introduction to the Art and Science of Understanding and Shaping Tomorrow's World.* Washington, D.C.: World Future Society.

Cronbach, L. J. 1951. "Coefficient Alpha and the Internal Structure of Tests." *Psychometrika* 16, pp. 297-334.

Davis, Kenneth Culp. 1971. *Discretionary Justice: A Preliminary Inquiry.* Urbana, Illinois: University of Illinois Press.

Dean, James W., and Brass, Daniel J. 1985. " Social Interaction and the Perception of Job Characteristics in an Organization." *Human Relations* 38, no. 6, pp. 571-582.

Decision Research. 1987. "Police-Community Relations Survey Report." San Diego, California: Robert Meadow.

Doig, Jameson W., and Hargrove, Erwin C. 1987. *Leadership and Innovation: A Biographical Perspective on Entrepreneurs in Government.* Baltimore, Maryland: The Johns Hopkins University Press.

Droge, Edward F., Jr. 1973. *The Patrolman: A Cop's Story.* New York: New American Library.

Drucker, Peter F. 1964. *Managing For Results.* New York: Harper and Row.

_____. 1973. *Management: Tasks, Responsibilities, Practices.* New York: Harper and Row.

Fiedler, Fred E., and Chemers, Martin M. 1974. *Leadership and Effective Management.* Glenview, Illinois: Scott, Foresman and Company.

Fisher, Roger, and Ury, William. 1981. *Getting to Yes: Negotiating Agreement Without Giving In.* Boston: Houghton Mifflin.

Fogelson, Robert M. 1977. *Big-City Police.* Cambridge, Massachusetts: Harvard University Press.

Forrester, Jay W. 1981. "Innovation in Economic Change." *Futures*, 13, pp. 323-331.

Fosdick, Raymond B. 1969. *American Police Systems.* 1920 Reprint. Montclair, New Jersey: Patterson Smith.

Fraser, Donald M. 1985. "Politics and Police Leadership: The View from City Hall." In *Police Leadership in America: Crisis and Opportunity.* Edited by William A. Geller. New York: Praeger.

Freeman, F. H. 1986. Review of *Thinking in Time: The Uses of History for Decision Makers* by Richard E. Neustadt and Ernest R. Mays. *Issues & Observations* 6, p. 5.

French, J. R. P., and Raven, B. 1959. "The Basis of Social Power." In *Studies in Social Power.* Edited by Dorwin Cartwright. Ann Arbor, Michigan: University of Michigan Press.

Fritz, Robert. 1984. *The Path of Least Resistance.* Salem, Massachusetts: DMA, Inc.

Fyfe, James F. 1985. *Police Management Today: Issues and Case Studies.* Washington, D.C.: International City Management Association.

Garmire, Bernard L., ed. 1982. *Local Government Police Management.* Washington, D.C.: International City Management Association.

Geller, William A., ed. 1983. "Police Misconduct: Scope of the Problem and Remedies." *American Bar Foundation Research Reported* 23 (Fall).

_____. 1985. *Police Leadership in America: Crisis and Opportunity.* New York: Praeger.

Ghiselin, Bernie. 1986. "Images." Interview with John Gardner. *Issues & Observations* 5, pp. 7-9.

_____. 1987a. "Images." From panel discussion with Warren G. Bennis. Issues & Observations 7, pp. 8-9.

_____. 1987b. "Risk, Adventure, and the Management of Self." Issues & Observations 7, no. 4 (Fall), pp. 1-5.

Goffman, Erving. 1959. *The Presentation of Self in Everday Life.* Garden City, New York: Doubleday Anchor.

Goldstein, Herman. 1975. *Police Corruption: A Perspective on Its Nature and Control.* Washington, D.C.: Police Foundation.

_____. 1977. *Policing a Free Society.* Cambridge, Massachusetts: Ballinger Publishing Company.

Guyot, Dorothy. 1979. "Bending Granite: Attempts to Change the Rank Structure of American Police Departments." *Journal of Police Science and Administration* 7, pp. 253-284.

Greenleaf, Robert. K. 1973. *The Servant as Leader.* Newton Center, Massachusetts: Robert K. Greenleaf Center.

Hersey, Paul. 1984. *The Situational Leader.* New York: Warner Books.

Hickman, Craig R., and Silva, Michael A. 1984. *Creating Excellence.* New York: New American Library.

Hsu, Cheng-Kuang, and Marsh, Robert M. 1983. "An Examination of the Determinants of Organizational Structure." *American Journal of Sociology* 88, no. 5 (March), pp. 975-996.

Hudnut, William H., III. 1985. "The Police and the Polis: A Mayor's Perspective." In *Police Leadership in America: Crisis and Opportunity.* Edited by William A. Geller. New York: Praeger.

Hunsaker, Phillip L., and Alessandra, Anthony J. 1980. *The Art of Managing People.* New York: Simon and Schuster.

Iannone, Nathan F. 1987. *Supervision of Police Personnel.* 4th rev. ed. Englewood Cliffs, New Jersey: Prentice-Hall.

Jablin, Fredric. 1982. "Formal Structural Characteristics of Organizations and Superior-Subordinate Communication." *Human Communication Research* 8, no. 4 (Summer), pp. 338-347.

Jago, Arthur G. 1981. "An Assessment of the Deemed Appropriateness of Participative Decision Making for High and Low Hierarchical Levels." *Human Relations* 34, no. 5, pp. 379-396.

Jankowicz, A. D. 1987. "Whatever Became of George Kelly? Applications and Implications." *American Psychologist* 42, no. 5 (May), pp. 481-487.

Johnson, D. W., and Johnson, R. T. 1983. "The Socialization and Achievement Crises: Are Cooperative Learning Experiences the Solution?" In *Applied Social Psychology Annual 4*. Beverly Hills, California: Sage Publications.

Juris, Hervey A. 1971. "The Implications of Police Unionism." *Law and Society Review* 6, no. 2 (November), pp. 231-242.

Kaplan, Robert E. 1986. "Implementing Strategy: Developing Organizations and Executives Together." *Issues & Observations* 6, no. 3 (Fall), pp. 1-5.

Kasperson, Conrad J. 1985. "An Exploration of the Relationship Between Performance, Decision-Making and Structure." *Human Relations* 38, no. 5, pp. 441-456.

Kauffman, Draper L. 1980. *Systems One: An Introduction to Systems Thinking*. Minneapolis, Minnesota: Future Systems, Inc.

Kelling, George L. 1985. "Justifying the Moral Propriety of Experimentation: A Case Study." In *Police Leadership in America: Crisis and Opportunity*. Edited by William A. Geller. New York: Praeger.

Kelling, George L., et al. 1974. *The Kansas City Preventive Patrol Experiment: A Technical Report*. Washington, D.C.: Police Foundation.

Kerlinger, Fred N. 1986. *Foundations of Behavioral Research*. 3d rev. ed. New York: Holt, Rinehart and Winston.

Kerstetter, Wayne A. 1985. "Who Disciplines the Police? Who Should?" In *Police Leadership in America: Crisis and Opportunity.* Edited by William A. Geller. New York: Praeger.

Kiefer, Charles, and Senge, Peter. 1984. "Metanoic Organizations." *In Transforming Work: A Collection of Organizational Transformation Readings,* Edited by John D. Adams. Alexandria, Virginia: Miles River Press.

Kiefer, Charles, and Stroh, Peter. 1984. "A New Paradigm for Developing Organizations." In *Transforming Work: A Collection of Organizational Transformation Readings.* Edited by John D. Adams. Alexandria, Virginia: Miles River Press.

Klockars, Carl B. 1985. "Order Maintenance, the Quality of Urban Life, and Police: A Different Line of Argument." In *Police Leadership in America: Crisis and Opportunity.* Edited by William A. Geller. New York: Praeger.

The Knapp Commission Report on Police Corruption. 1973. New York: George Braziller.

Kohn, Melvin L., and Schooler, Carmi. 1982. "Job Conditions and Personality: A Longitudinal Assessment of Their Reciprocal Effects." *American Journal of Sociology* 87, no. 6 (May), pp. 1257-1286.

Kouzes, James M., and Posner, Barry Z. 1987. *The Leadership Challenge: How to Get Extraordinary Things Done in Organizations.* San Francisco: Jossey-Bass.

Kubler-Ross, Elisabeth. 1969. *On Death and Dying.* New York: Macmillan.

Langworthy, Robert H. 1986. *The Structure of Police Organizations*. New York: Praeger.

Lauer, Robert H. 1982. *Perspectives on Social Change*. 3d rev. ed. Boston: Allyn and Bacon, Inc.

Lauer, Robert H., and Handel, Warren H. 1983. *Social Psychology: The Theory and Application of Symbolic Interactionism*. 2d rev. ed. Englewood Cliffs, New Jersey: Prentice-Hall.

Leinen, Stephen. 1984. *Black Police, White Society*. New York: New York University Press.

Leonard, V. A., and More, Harry W. 1971. *Police Organization and Management*. 3d rev. ed. Mineola, New York: The Foundation Press.

Lerner, Max. 1987. "The Total Person in Social Context." Graduate seminar, United States International University, San Diego, California.

Lipsky, Michael, ed. 1970. *Law and Order: Police Encounters*. New Brunswick, New Jersey: Aldine Publishing Company.

Lord, Lesli Kay. 1983. "A Comparison of Male and Female Peace Officers' Stereotypic Perceptions of Women and Women Peace Officers." Ph.D. dissertation, United States International University, San Diego.

Luthans, Fred. 1985. *Organizational Behavior*. 4th rev. ed. New York: McGraw-Hill.

Maas, Peter. 1973. *Serpico: The Cop Who Defied the System*. New York: Viking Press.

Manning, Peter K., Van Maanen, John. 1978. *Policing: A View From the Street*. Santa Monica, California: Goodyear Publishing Company.

Mayo, Louis A. 1985. "Leading Blindly: An Assessment of Chiefs' Information About Police Operations." In *Police Leadership in America: Crisis and Opportunity.* Edited by William A. Geller. New York: Praeger.

McClure, James. 1984. *Cop World: Inside an American Police Force.* New York: Pantheon Books.

McGregor, Douglas. 1960. *The Human Side of Enterprise.* New York: McGraw-Hill.

McKnight, Richard. 1984. "Spirituality in the Workplace." In *Transforming Work: A Collection of Organizational Transformation Readings.* Edited by John D. Adams. Alexandria, Virginia: Miles River Press.

McNamara, Donal E. J. 1985. "Discipline in American Policing." In *The Ambivalent Force: Perspectives on the Police.* Edited by Abraham S. Blumberg and Elaine Niederhoffer. New York: Holt, Rinehart, and Winston.

Milgram, Stanley. 1974. *Obedience to Authority.* New York: Harper and Row.

Milton, Catherine. 1972. *Women in Policing.* Washington, D.C.: Police Foundation.

Mintzberg, Henry. 1980. *The Nature of Managerial Work.* Englewood Cliffs, New Jersey: Prentice-Hall.

Mitchell, Terence R., and Scott, William G. 1987. "Leadership Failures, the Distrusting Public, and Prospects of the Administrative State." *Public Administration Review* 47, no. 6 (November/December), pp. 445-452.

Moore, Mark H., and Kelling, George L. 1983. "To Serve and Protect: Learning from Police History." *The Public Interest* 70 (Winter), pp. 49-65.

Moore, R. 1983. "Strategies for Increasing the Number of Black Police Executives." *FBI Law Enforcement Bulletin* 52, no. 6 (June), pp. 14-20.

More, Harry W., Jr. 1981. *Critical Issues in Law Enforcement.* 3d rev. ed. Cincinnati: Anderson Publishing.

Morris, Norval. 1985. Foreword to *Police Leadership in America: Crisis and Opportunity.* Edited by William A. Geller. New York: Praeger.

Muir, William Ker, Jr. 1977. *Police: Streetcorner Politicians.* Chicago: The University of Chicago Press.

Munro, Jim L. 1974. *Administrative Behavior and Police Organization.* Cincinnati, Ohio: The W. H. Anderson Company.

Murphy, Patrick V. 1985. "The Prospective Chief's Negotiation of Authority with the Mayor." In *Police Leadership in America: Crisis and Opportunity.* Edited by William A. Geller. New York: Praeger.

Naisbitt, John. 1982. *Megatrends: Ten New Directions Transforming Our Lives.* New York: Warner Books.

National Advisory Commission on Criminal Justice Standards and Goals. 1973. Washington, D.C.: United States Government Printing Office.

National Commission on the Causes and Prevention of
Violence. 1968. *Rights in Conflict: A Report
Submitted by Daniel Walker.* New York: Signet
Books.

National Commission on Law Observance and Enforcement,
Lawlessness in Law Enforcement. 1931. *Report
on Police.* 1968 Reprint. Montclair, New Jersey:
Patterson Smith.

Niederhoffer, Arthur. 1969. *Behind the Shield: The Police in
Urban Society.* Garden City, New York: Anchor
Books.

Officer Safety Task Force. 1985. "Officer Safety Task Force:
Final Report." San Diego, California: San Diego
Police Department.

Ouchi, William. 1981. *Theory Z: How American Business
Can Meet the Japanese Challenge.* Reading,
Massachusetts: Addison Wesley.

Pascale, Richard Tanner, and Athos, Anthony G. 1981. *The
Art of Japanese Management: Applications for
American Executives.* New York: Warner Books.

Peters, Thomas J. 1984. *A Passion for Excellence.* Film.

Peters, Thomas J., and Waterman, Robert H., Jr. 1982. *In
Search of Excellence: Lessons From America's
Best-Run Companies.* New York: Harper and Row.

Portnoy, Robert A. 1986. *Leadership! What Every Leader
Should Know About People.* Englewood Cliffs,
New Jersey: Prentice-Hall.

President's Commission on Law Enforcement and the
Administration of Justice. 1967. *The Challenge of
Crime in a Free Society*: Washington, D.C.: United
States Government Printing Office.

Punch, M. 1983. *Control in the Police Organization.* Cambridge, Massachusetts: MIT Press.

_____., ed. 1985. *Conduct Unbecoming: The Social Construction of Police Deviance and Control.* New York: Methuen, Inc.

Quinney, Richard. 1970. *The Social Reality of Crime.* Boston: Little, Brown and Company.

_____. 1975. *Criminology: Analysis and Critique of Crime in America.* Boston: Little, Brown and Company.

Reeves, Goebel. 1961. "Hobo's Lullaby." New York: Fall River Music Inc.

Reiss, Albert J. 1971. *The Police and the Public.* New Haven, Connecticut: Yale University Press.

_____. 1985. "Shaping and Serving the Community: The Role of the Police Chief Executive." In *Police Leadership in America: Crisis and Opportunity.* Edited by William A. Geller. New York: Praeger.

Reuss-Ianni, E. 1983. *Two Cultures of Policing: Street Cops and Management Cops.* New Brunswick, New Jersey: Transaction Books.

Richardson, James F. 1970. *The New York Police: Colonial Times to 1901.* New York: Oxford University Press.

Richmond, Virginia; McCroskey, James; and Davis, Leonard M. 1982. "Individual Differences Among Employees, Management Communication Style, and Employee Satisfaction: Replication and Extension." *Human Communication Research* 8, no. 2 (Winter), pp. 170-188.

Ritscher, James A. 1986. "Spiritual Leadership." In *Transforming Leadership: From Vision to Results.* Edited by John D. Adams. Alexandria, Virginia: Miles River Press.

Roberg, Roy R. 1976. *The Changing Police Role: New Dimensions and New Issues.* San Jose, California: Justice Systems Development.

_____. 1979. *Police Management and Organizational Behavior: A Contingency Approach.* St. Paul, Minnesota: West Publishing.

Ross, Richard. 1987. "Leadership, Mastery, and Systems Thinking." Management team workshop, San Diego Police Department, Fallbrook, California.

Rubin, Herbert J. 1983. *Applied Social Research.* Columbus, Ohio: Charles E. Merrill.

Rubinstein, Jonathan. 1973. *City Police.* New York: Farrar, Straus and Giroux.

Rumbaut, Ruben G. 1977. "The Politics of Reform in a Police Bureaucracy: A Case Study in Social Intervention and Organizational Change." Ph.D. dissertation, Brandeis University, Waltham, Massachusetts.

Rumbaut, Ruben G., and Bittner, Egon. 1979. "Changing Conceptions of the Police Role: A Sociological Review." In *Crime and Justice: An Annual Review of Research.* Chicago: The University of Chicago Press.

Rumbaut, Ruben, and Stamper, Norman H. 1974. *Community Profiling and Police Patrol: Final Staff Report of the Community Profile Development Project.* San Diego: San Diego Police Department.

Schein, Edgar H. 1969. *Process Consultation.* Reading, Massachusetts: Addison-Wesley.

_____. 1985. *Organizational Culture and Leadership: A Dynamic View.* San Francisco: Jossey-Bass, Inc.

Schmidt, Wayne W. 1985. "Section 1983 and the Changing Face of Police Management." In *Police Leadership in America: Crisis and Opportunity.* Edited by William A. Geller. New York: Praeger.

Schutz, 1958. *FIRO: A Three Dimensional Theory of Interpersonal Behavior.* New York: Holt, Rinehart and Winston.

Scott, Michael S. 1986. *Managing for Success: A Police Chief's Survival Guide.* Washington, D.C.: Police Executive Research Forum.

Shapard, John E. 1985. "The Ethics of Experimentation in Law Enforcement." In *Police Leadership in America: Crisis and Opportunity.* Edited by William A. Geller. New York: Praeger.

Shaw, Marvin E. 1981. *Group Dynamics: The Psychology of Small Group Behavior.* New York: McGraw-Hill.

Sherman, Lawrence W. 1985. "The Police Executive as Statesman." In *Police Leadership in America: Crisis and Opportunity.* Edited by William A. Geller. New York: Praeger.

Shev, Edward E., and Hewes, Jeremy Joan. 1977. *Good Cops/Bad Cops: Memoirs of a Police Psychiatrist.* San Francisco: San Francisco Book Company.

Silberman, Charles E. 1978. *Criminal Violence, Criminal Justice.* New York: Random House.

Skolnick, Jerome H. 1966. *Justice Without Trial: Law Enforcement in Democratic Society.* New York: John Wiley and Sons.

Skolnick, Jerome H., and Bayley, David H. 1986. *The New Blue Line: Police Innovations in Six American Cities.* New York: The Free Press.

Skolnick, Jerome H., and Gray, Thomas C. 1975. *Police in America.* Boston: Little, Brown and Company.

Skolnick, Jerome H., and McCoy, Candace. 1985. "Police Accountability and the Media." In *Police Leadership in America: Crisis and Opportunity.* Edited by William A. Geller. New York: Praeger.

Skousen, W. Cleon. 1977. *Notes for the New Chief: A Police Chief's Manual.* New York: Law and Order.

Smith, Bruce. 1940. *Police Systems in the United States.* New York: Harper and Brothers.

Sorcher, Melvin. 1985. *Predicting Executive Success: What It Takes To Make It Into Senior Management.* New York: John Wiley and Sons.

Spencer, Herbert. 1971. In *Herbert Spencer: Structure, Function and Evolution.* Edited by Stanislav Andreski. New York: Charles Scribner's Sons.

Spier, Morris S. 1988. Personal Interview, San Diego, California. 4 February.

Srivastva, Suresh, et al. ed. 1984. *The Executive Mind.* San Francisco: Jossey-Bass Publishing.

_____. 1986. *Executive Power.* San Francisco: Jossey-Bass Publishing.

Stamper, Norman H. 1976. *San Diego's Community Oriented Policing: A Case Study in Organizational Change.* San Diego: San Diego Police Department.

_____. 1977. *An Investigation into Allegations of Racial Prejudice and Discriminatory Police Practices in Southeast San Diego.* San Diego: San Diego Police Department.

_____. 1986. "An Experience of Change: Self Help." Unpublished paper. San Diego, California.

Stamper, Norman H., et al. 1981. *Crime and Justice in San Diego: Report of the Mayor's Crime Control Commission.* San Diego, California: City of San Diego.

Stern, Alfred. 1967. *Sartre: His Philosophy and Existential Psychoanalysis.* 2d rev. ed. New York: Dell Publishing Company.

Swanson, Charles R., and Territo, Leonard. 1983. *Police Administration: Structures, Processes, and Behavior.* New York: Macmillan.

Sweeney, Thomas J., and Ellingsworth, William. 1973. *Issues in Police Patrol: A Book of Readings.* Washington, D.C.: Police Foundation.

Tafoya, William L. 1986. "A Delphi Forecast of the Future of Law Enforcement." Ph.D. dissertation, University of Maryland, College Park, Maryland.

Task Force on Human Relations Training. 1986. Report on the San Diego Police Department Human Relations Training Program. San Diego, California: San Diego Police Department.

Taylor, Frederick W. 1947. *Scientific Management.* New York: Harper and Brothers.

Terkel, Studs. 1975. *Working: People Talk About What They Do All Day and How They Feel About What They Do.* New York: Random House.

Tetlock, Philip E. 1985. "Accountability: The Neglected Social Context of Judgment and Choice." *Research in Organizational Behavior* 7, pp. 297-332.

Thompson, George J., and Stroud, Michael J. 1984. *Verbal Judo.* Albuquerque, New Mexico: The Verbal Judo Institute.

Tjosvold, Dean. 1984. "Cooperation Theory and Organizations." *Human Relations* 37, no. 9, pp. 743-767.

Toch, Hans; Grant, J. Douglas; and Galvin, Raymond T. 1975. *Agents of Change: A Study in Police Reform.* New York: John Wiley and Sons.

Toffler, Alvin. 1970. *Future Shock.* New York: Random House.

Townsend, Robert. 1984. *Further Up the Organization: How to Stop Management from Stifling People and Strangling Productivity.* New York: Alfred A. Knopf.

U.S. Congress House Subcommittee on Criminal Justice. 1984. Report on Hearings in New York City on Police Misconduct. Rockville, Maryland: National Criminal Justice Reference Service.

Vollmer, August. 1936. *The Police and Modern Society.* Berkeley, California: University of California Press.

Walker, Samuel. 1985. "Setting the Standards: The Efforts and Impact of Blue-Ribbon Commissions on the Police." In *Police Leadership in America: Crisis and Opportunity.* Edited by William A. Geller. New York: Praeger.

Walker, T. Mike. 1969. *Voices From the Bottom of the World: A Policeman's Journal.* New York: Evergreen Black Cat.

Wambaugh, Joseph. 1970. *The New Centurions.* Boston: Little, Brown.

_____. 1972. *Blue Knight.* Boston: G. K. Hall.

Weber, Max. 1946. *From Max Weber: Essays in Sociology.* Edited by H. H. Gerth and C. Wright Mills. New York: Oxford University Press.

Webster's New Collegiate Dictionary. 1979. S.v. "Paramilitary."

Weisbord, M. R. 1976. "Organizational Diagnosis: Six Places to Look for Trouble With or Without a Theory." *Group and Organizational Studies: The International Journal for Group Facilitators 1,* no. 4, pp. 430-447.

Westley, William A. 1970. *Violence and the Police: A Sociological Study of Law, Custom and Morality.* Cambridge, Massachusetts: MIT Press.

Wheelis, Allen. 1973. *How People Change.* New York: Harper and Row.

Whittemore, L. H. 1969. *Cop! A Closeup of Violence and Tragedy.* Greenwich, Connecticut: Fawcett Publications.

Williams, Hubert. 1985. "Retrenchment, the Constitution, and Policing." In *Police Leadership in America: Crisis and Opportunity.* Edited by William A. Geller. New York: Praeger.

Williamson, John N. 1984. *The Leader-Manager.* Eden Praire, Minnesota: Wilson Learning Group.

Wilson, James Q., and Herrnstein, Richard J. 1985. *Crime and Human Nature.* New York: Simon and Schuster.

Wilson, James Q., and Kelling, George L. 1982. "Police and Neighborhood Safety: Broken Windows." *Atlantic Monthly* 249 (March), pp. 29-38.

Wilson, O. W., and McLaren, Roy C. 1972. *Police Administration.* 3d ed. New York: McGraw-Hill.

Witham, Donald C. 1985. *The American Law Enforcement Chief Executive: A Management Profile.* Washington, D.C.: Police Executive Research Forum.

_____. 1987. "Transformational Police Leadership." *FBI Law Enforcement Bulletin* 56, no. 12, pp. 2-6.

Yates, Douglas, Jr. 1985. *The Politics of Management.* San Francisco: Jossey-Bass Publishers.

Zaleznik, Abraham. 1983. "Managers and Leaders: Are They Different?" In *Executive Success.* New York: John Wiley and Sons.

Zenger, John H. 1985. "Leadership: Management's Better Half." *Training* (December), pp. 44-53.

Appendix A

TECHNICAL DISCUSSION OF RESEARCH METHODOLOGY AND SURVEY RESPONSES

If you want to know what people think,
why not ask them? They might just tell
you.
　　　　　—A. D. Jankowicz, quoting
　　　　　George Kelly (1987:481)

A decision was made early in the planning stages of this research to attempt to learn how big-city police chiefs view and approach their day-to-day work. Another early decision was simply to *ask* them. This was accomplished by inviting them to express their opinions about a wide range of organizational and community concerns. Those opinions, it was theorized, might be used to examine both the explicit and implicit values the chiefs attach to their roles in general as well as to their specific executive leadership and executive management functions. To learn whether these same executives behave generally in accordance with their professed values, their immediate subordinates were asked to describe—but not evaluate—their bosses' actual performance.

Research Design

The study employed two survey instruments (questionnaires), each designed by the researcher (see Appendix B) and collectively called the police leadership practices survey (PLPS). Developed to help answer the research questions presented in Chapter One, the PLPS was tailored to the two respondent populations: the chief executives and their immediate subordinates, hereinafter referred to as "assistants." All respondents were asked to complete a demographic and biographical information cover sheet and then to answer the 100-item questionnaires. The only difference in the two survey instruments is that the chiefs were asked to record their professed values, while the assistants "responding to identical survey items" were asked to record observations of their chiefs' actual behavior. Complete confidentiality was promised to all respondents.

Subjects of the Study

Originally, the 46 members of the nationwide Major Cities Police Chiefs Association and 92 of their assistants were selected as the principal subjects of the study. This decision was based on the belief that members of that professional association, representing all but a few of the largest police departments in the country, would be willing to cooperate with a study whose purpose was consistent with their association's *raison d'etre*. Further, the researcher's own chief executive chaired the Major Cities Police Chiefs Association at the time of the study, and he was willing to use his influence to help yield a high return on the survey. To this end, a letter from the chair was sent to all members of the association asking for their assistance.

A decision was made later, however, to enlarge the study's population because (1) not all large U.S. cities are represented in the Major Cities Police Chiefs Association, and (2) even with a high rate of return on the survey, the population would still be relatively small. Therefore, surveys were sent to *all* big American police departments headed by an appointed chief executive—except for the researcher's own organization, the San Diego Police Department. "Big" is defined somewhat arbitrarily in the context of this research as a police department in a city of at least 200,000 population. Implicit in the theoretical orientation of the study is the notion that distinctions between leadership and management functions may be more difficult, if not impossible, to discern in smaller police agencies.

Questionnaires were sent to a total of 216 potential respondents: 72 police chiefs and 144 assistants who reported directly to their chiefs. Two "assistant" questionnaires were sent to each agency, a decision based on a desire to capture more than one assistant's perceptions of his or her boss's behavior. The color-coded surveys were mailed in one envelope to the chief executives, who were asked to distribute the appropriate survey instruments to assistants of their own choosing. Separate return envelopes were included for each survey instrument, along with instructions intended to maintain the integrity of the data.

Because the entire universe (of police departments serving cities with populations of 200,000 or more) was surveyed, there is no sample population. Representativeness of the chief executives, therefore, is not an issue in this study. The representativeness of those reporting directly to the police chiefs, however, may be a problem. For logistical reasons, only two copies of the "assistant" survey instrument were sent to each agency. The number of surbordinates reporting directly to the chief executives varies widely; some chiefs have only one immediate assistant while others may have several. Therefore, the question of the representativeness of the assistant population, while unsettled, might be resolved as a product of the relatively large sample size (N=92).

Instrumentation

A search for existing instrumentation that would permit the collection and analysis of data needed to answer the research questions proved futile. While numerous survey instruments can be used to define or assess leadership or management "style," there appears to be no instrument that addresses directly the distinction between executive leadership and executive management. This is particularly true for the law enforcement setting. More specifically, the researcher was seeking a means of capturing the extent to which police chief executives discern a difference between the two functions, as well as the extent to which they act on those differences.

Rejection of Existing Survey Instruments

Considered and rejected were Blake and Mouton's managerial grid (Bass, 1981); Bradford and Cohen's (1984) "Leadership Style Questionnaire"; Hersey and Blanchard's (Hersey, 1984) "Situational Leader" model; and Kouzes and Posner's (1987) "Leadership Practices Inventory." The purpose of the present research was not to assess executive qualities or styles, such as "autocratic," "democratic," "trusting," or "controlling." The focus, briefly put, was rather more narrow: Do big-city police chiefs see and act upon differences between the leadership function and the management function?

The New Instrument

The PLPS was developed for use in the study. Its design followed the researcher's creation of a leadership-management typology, which defines each executive function in ideal terms and as polar extremes. These two types, leader and manager, were then placed conceptually at the two ends of a continuum, and three gradients, or additional types, were created: leader-manager, centrist, and manager-leader. Next, definitions were developed for each position on the continuum (see Glossary). As will be discussed later, the "centrist" position was eventually deleted for purposes of survey construction.

Inspiration for the Model

The conceptual executive "types"—leader, leader-manager, manager-leader, and manager—were intended to anticipate and to help explain evidence of the *behavioral* orientations of the police chief subjects of this study. Inspiration for their creation was drawn from the experience of the researcher's 22 years in the San Diego Police Department and his work as a consultant to over 30 other law enforcement agencies. Also contributing to the theoretical foundation of the leader-through-manager model are the writings of several researchers and observers.

Classification of Functions

Following the creation of the leader-through-manager conceptual model, the researcher began a process of generating on 3 x 5-inch cards a wide range of tasks, duties, responsibilities, values, and behaviors that could be classified according to the model. Those cards containing descriptions of leader behavior, or implicit leader *functions*, were placed under the leader heading; those containing descriptions of manager functions were placed under the manager heading, and so forth. Approximately 200 such cards were ultimately completed and classified. From this material, the PLPS was eventually created.

The items, or "variables" (eventually reduced to 100 through a process of eliminating excessive redundancies), were constructed to elicit a response from "strongly agree" to "strongly disagree" on a five-point scale. An example of a statement (that is, a variable or item) in the chiefs' version is "I believe the police chief executive should invite citizen input on agency policies." The same item in the assistants' version reads, "I perceive that my boss invites citizen input on agency policies." A "5" indicates full agreement; a "1" indicates complete disagreement.

Research Procedures

When, through a process of subjective review (including discussions with numerous colleagues), the number of variables had been reduced from 200 to 125 the researcher conducted a preliminary "field test" of the instruments. Eleven colleagues completed the survey. This early exercise was not intended to establish content validity but (1) to learn whether the items were unambiguous and easily comprehensible and (2) to determine how long it would take the respondents to complete the questionnaires. The feedback was immediate. Each questionnaire took an average of 10 minutes to complete (the range was from 5 to 19 minutes); the items were perceived as generally very clear; and the experience was described as "fun," "interesting," and "easy."

Responding to criticisms and suggestions, the researcher eliminated excessive redundancies and ambiguities thereby reducing the number of items on the survey instruments to 100. At this point, 20 items had been formulated for each of the original five positions in the leader-through-manager model.

Content Validation

The PLPS was then mailed to the first of two *expert panels,* whose members had agreed to assist in establishing content validity of the survey. This first panel (external) was composed of five active and respected researchers, consultants, and trainers in the field of organizational leadership and management. The second was a two-person panel (internal) and consisted of the chief of police and the assistant chief of police of the San Diego Police Department.

According to Kerlinger (1986:417),

> Content validity is the *representativeness* or *sampling adequacy* of the content—the substance, the matter, the topic—of a measuring instrument. *Content* validation is guided by the question: Is the substance or content of this measure representative of the content or the universe of content of the property being measured?

Because content validation "consists essentially in *judgment*" (Kerlinger, 1986:418), it was essential to expose the newly developed PLPS to a critical analysis by respected experts both in the general field of leadership and management and in the particular field of police executive leadership.

The "external" experts. As mentioned, the PLPS was first mailed to the external panel of subject-matter experts for review. Panelists completed the survey independently. Upon completion of this step, a workshop of the subject matter experts was convened and the panelists were asked to (1) judge the meaning and the clarity of each item; (2) classify, from their individual points of view, each item according to the leader-through-manager model; and (3) recommend modifications to the survey instrument or, for that matter, to the research design.

This workshop experience, combined with consultations with research methodologists, resulted in a decision to proceed with a slightly revised survey construction. The new design was still intended to capture respondents' answers across the five-point scale from "strongly agree" to "strongly disagree," but it now called for the use of 25 "leader" and 25 "manager" items, rather than the original 20 for each. The "leader-manager" and "manager-leader" positions on the continuum were also increased to 25 items each, while the "centrist" position was dropped.

The external panel was in agreement that the use of three gradients (as opposed to two) between the polar extremes of leader and manager tended to create artificial distinctions within that range of responses. Moreover, because this study sought to determine the extent to which chief executives operationalize a distinction between the two poles of *leadership* and *management*, it was felt that the conversion—at least conceptually—of the remaining "middle ground" of 25 leader-manager and 25 manager-leader items into "fillers" or "distracters" would be appropriate. In short, the survey would seek primarily to discern differences in the *fundamental* orientations of American police chiefs. Are they principally oriented toward leadership functions, toward management functions, or toward a blending of the two?

The effect of eliminating the "centrist" position, it was argued, would be to bring more clearly into relief any discernible differences the police chiefs manifest—either in professed values or in observed behavior—in approaching the two functions of executive leadership and executive management.

The external expert panel also served as willing subjects of a pretest, identifying a total of 16 items that needed to be clarified, modified, or replaced. This work was done before the PLPS was typed in final form and prepared for distribution.

The police expert panel. Readied for distribution, but not yet mailed, the PLPS was administered to the two-person police expert panel. The police chief completed the version designed to capture his professed values, and the assistant chief completed the version intended to provide his perceptions of the observed behavior of his boss. Based on the researcher's rather intimate knowledge of the two officials, it was concluded that the survey instrument had passed its final, albeit highly subjective, test; significantly, there were literally no surprises in the responses of either of those professionals.

Survey Distribution

Once ready for distribution, a letter to all police chief respondents (including but not limited to members of the Major Cities Police Chiefs Association) was drafted for the San Diego police chief's signature and mailed. The letter to his colleagues alerted them to the purpose of the research, asked for their support and cooperation, and promised them confidentiality. One week later, the PLPS was mailed to the chiefs. A separate stamped, self-addressed envelope was

included for each respondent, with discrete, sequential identification numbers having been affixed to each survey instrument. Respondents were informed that they would receive a
summary of the results if they were interested, and a survey request form was included to accommodate their desire.

Data Analysis, Assumption, and Limitations

This research sought to answer the four questions raised in
Chapter One. Briefly summarized, the questions were intended to generate information about the organizational and
community values of big-city American police chiefs; relationships between the police chiefs and their assistants; views and
practices that relate to the functions of executive leadership
and executive management; and differences between or among
leaders that may be attributable to agency size, education level,
or age of the chief executive, or any other demographic or
biographical considerations. The principal concern was
whether police chief executives profess a commitment to their
leadership functions and whether, as viewed by their immediate subordinates, their actual practices conform to those expressed values.

Data Analysis

As nonexperimental research, the present study had no
hypotheses and, strictly construed, no independent and dependent variables. It was, however, intended to produce a huge
volume of nominal-level data and the prospect of great
variability. The methods of analysis, then, had to be useful in
"determining whether apparent differences in bivariate table
values are real or due to chance" (Rubin, 1983:428). Selected
for use in analyzing the data were reliability and factor
analyses, correlations between scales and subscales (which had
surfaced as serendipitous effects of a rotated factor analysis),
correlations between items (or variables) and scales and subscales, and frequency distributions of results for both individual

variables and scales and subscales. Finally, *t* tests were conducted to determine the significance of difference, if any, between the respondents' scores on the leadership versus the management scales.

Assumption

The researcher made the assumption that respondents in this survey answered the questionnaire honestly and as accurately as limitations in human perception and human communication allow. This assumption was predicated on a belief that the survey population consisted of people who were dedicated to the continuing advancement of the profession.

Limitations

One limitation of this study was that the survey procedure has an inherent tendency to remove temporarily the respondents from their social context. As the individual sits at his or her desk completing the questionnaire, the very act of the exercise can, for example, produce responses that reflect one's view of how things ought to be rather than how one actually perceives them to be. Recent or impending events in the life of the organization or of the individual could have a significant bearing on the mood and, consequently, the responses of those surveyed. The shooting death of an officer, for example, could profoundly affect answers to specific items on this particular instrument.

Another potential challenge was that, because the researcher was in the same field as the respondents, there could have been a tendency to answer in accord with what the respondents thought a colleague might want to hear. (Conversely, it is also possible that even an unknown colleague could have been given straightforward answers that might be denied the "outsider.")

The method of administering the survey instruments posed potential problems. To demonstrate and elicit trust, all copies of the PLPS were mailed directly to the chief executives. But, despite several promises of confidentiality and the use of separate return envelopes, the possibility exists that (1) respondents, for personal reasons, may have feared disclosure of critical opinions; (2) the chief executives did not give copies to their subordinates; (3) the chief executives may have actually delegated the task of completing their own surveys to a subordinate (itself a telling but ultimately undiscoverable phenomenon); or (4) the chief executives selected only those "loyal" subordinates who could be counted on to provide responses thought to be favorable to the boss.

Finally, the PLPS itself, having never been used before, presented a limitation. Despite a preliminary field test and the work of two "content validity" expert panels, there was no guarantee that the survey would accomplish its purpose of helping the researcher answer the research questions.

Agencies Responding and Not Responding to the PLPS

As previously noted, all U.S. cities of 200,000 or greater (with the exception of San Diego) and policed by an agency headed by an appointed chief executive were selected for the survey research—a total of 72 American cities. Responses were received from 55 (76 percent) of these cities. Twenty-eight states are represented. *Table A-1* lists those agencies from which at least one response was received. A total of three responses from each agency was possible—a total of 216 potential respondents, of whom 67 percent returned completed questionnaires. Of the 55 participating agencies, 43 (78 percent) returned a full three-respondent set of completed survey instruments.

Table A-1
Agencies Responding to the PLPS

	Agency	Chiefs	Assist's	Total		Agency	Chiefs	Assist's	Total
1.	Akron	1	2	3	29.	Mesa	1	2	3
2.	Albuquerque	1	2	3	30.	Miami	1	2	3
3.	Anaheim	1	2	3	31.	Milwaukee	1	2	3
4.	Anchorage	1	2	3	32.	Minneapolis	1	2	3
5.	Atlanta	1	2	3	33.	Mobile	1	2	3
6.	Austin	1	0	1	34.	Nashville	1	1	2
7.	Aurora	1	2	3	35.	Newark	1	2	3
8.	Baton Rouge	1	2	3	36.	Oakland	1	2	3
9.	Birmingham	1	2	3	37.	OK City	1	2	3
10.	Boston	1	2	3	38.	Omaha	1	2	3
11.	Buffalo	1	2	3	39.	Philadelphia	1	0	1
12.	Cincinnati	1	1	2	40.	Phoenix	1	2	3
13.	Cleveland	1	2	3	41.	Pittsburgh	1	2	3
14.	CO Springs	1	2	3	42.	Portland	1	2	3
15.	Columbus	1	2	3	43.	Rochester	1	0	1
16.	Corpus Christi	1	2	3	44.	Sacramento	1	2	3
17.	Dallas	0	1	1	45.	St. Paul	1	2	3
18.	Denver	1	2	3	46.	Santa Ana	1	2	3
19.	Detroit	0	1	1	47.	San Jose	0	2	2
20.	Fort Worth	1	1	2	48.	San Antonio	1	2	3
21.	Fresno	1	1	2	49.	Seattle	1	2	3
22.	Houston	1	2	3	50.	Shreveport	1	0	1
23.	Indianapolis	1	2	3	51.	Tampa Bay	1	2	3
24.	Kansas City	1	2	3	52.	Tucson	1	2	3
25.	Lexington	1	1	2	53.	Tulsa	1	2	3
26.	Long Beach	1	2	3	54.	VA Beach	1	2	3
27.	Los Angeles	1	2	3	55.	Wash., D.C.	1	2	3
28.	Louisville	1	2	3					

As can be seen from *Table A-1*, responses were received from 52 chiefs and 95 assistants for a total of 147 respondents. A simple analysis of the data reveals that the incomplete response pattern—those cases in which only one or two of the three potential respondents of a given agency returned surveys—produced a random "cancellation" effect. That is, the pattern of incomplete data of one set of surveys returned by a particular city was generally offset by the "reverse" pattern of incomplete data returned by another (only three chiefs of those cities providing a response failed to return the survey, while in only five other cities was there no response from the assistants). Of course, had the aim of this study been to determine correlations of the opinions of chiefs versus assistants by specific agencies, elimination of those data sets in which only the chief or only the assistant(s) responded would have been required. Because that was not the case, all of the returned surveys were deemed useful to the study.

Demographic Characteristics of the Two Respondent Populations

An important consideration in interpreting the data from the PLPS was the extent to which variations in demographic or biographical characteristics of the two respondent populations (chiefs and their assistants) may have produced differential responses to the substantive questions, either within or between the two groups.

The big-city police chiefs who participated in this study are exclusively men, predominantly white (78 percent), and in their early 50s. They range in age from 40 to 72 (mean age is 50.2). Most have college degrees (mean years of education is 16.4), although the range in education is great. They have been in law enforcement for over a quarter of a century (mean is 26.6 years).

Analyses of PLPS Items and Scales

To review, this research began with a conceptual and theoretical framework that, supported by a growing body of literature, views leadership and management as discrete, discernible organizational functions. Further, it was observed that executive leadership and executive management may be seen as occupying opposite poles in a leader-manager continuum with "leader-manager" and "manager-leader" orientations serving as potentially distinguishable gradients along that continuum.

That theory guided the creation of the PLPS survey. A set of 25 survey items, or variables, was developed for each of the four scales of the leader-through-manager PLPS instrument. Specifically, respondents to the PLPS were offered a series of 100 statements and asked to indicate on a five-point scale the extent to which they agreed or disagreed with each. A "5" indicated maximum agreement; a "1," maximum disagreement; and "3," a neutral midpoint.

An important caution is in order: In the following discussion, descriptions of the survey items have been shortened quite severely to meet restrictions imposed by table format. (See Appendix B for full descriptions.)

Reliability Analysis

Following collection of the data, results were first put to a test of internal consistency; in other words, did each of the four scales of the PLPS assess reliably what they had been designed to assess?

Each of the four scales was subjected to reliability analysis using Cronbach's alpha (Cronbach, 1951).[*] As can be seen in *Table A-2*, each of the four alphas reflects exceptionally strong internal consistency, both for the overall sample as well as for the subsamples of chiefs and assistants. Thus, the overall reliability of the PLPS as a research instrument for assessing attitudes among and about big-city police chiefs appears to be remarkably solid.

Tables A-3–A-6 offer a more detailed breakdown of results for each of the four PLPS scales and their composing variables. Those tables present combined mean scores for the sample of chief executives and their assistants, as well as separate scores for each subsample. Included are the "item-to-total" correlations, which are ranked from high to low on the

---

[*]The Statistical Package for the Social Sciences (SPSS˟) was used in the analysis of all data in this research.

Table A-2

Reliability Coefficients (Cronbach's Alpha) for Each of the Four Scales of the PLPS

Scale	Alpha (Total)	Chiefs	Assistants
Leader	.898	.855	.906
Leader-Manager	.940	.877	.943
Manager-Leader	.903	.887	.912
Manager	.897	.909	.891

basis of the combined mean scores. That is, the tables show the corrected correlation of each *item* with the remaining 24 items composing the total scale. The higher the item-to-total correlation coefficient, the greater the significance of each item as an index of the executive leadership or executive management function measured by the overall scale; the lower the correlation, the lesser the perceived importance of a given item to the overall scale. As seen in each of the next four tables, the standard deviations for the *total* 25-item scale scores are considerably lower than individual item standard deviations. That reflects the degree of variance within each respondent's set of scores rather than between or among respondents.

With correlations at or above .5 viewed conventionally as quite robust, and with correlations in the range of .3 to .4 viewed as moderately robust, it is clear from *Tables A-3* through *A-6* that the PLPS has produced a defensible indication of how the populations of big-city police chiefs and their assistants view executive leadership and executive management functions.

Table A-3

Correlations of Items to Other Items Within the Leader Scale of the PLPS

Item	Description	Total (N=144)			Chiefs (N=52)			Assistants (N=92)		
		Mean	S.D.	Item-to-Total Corr.	Mean	S.D.	Item-to-Total Corr.	Mean	S.D.	Item-to-Total Corr.
81	Shared vision	4.24	.98	.704	4.61	.58	.534	3.94	1.12	.724
49	Celebrates	4.22	.81	.686	4.32	.71	.690	4.12	.88	.681
53	Recognizes	4.69	.60	.669	4.82	.39	.462	4.57	.69	.699
41	Acts as model	4.30	.94	.669	4.50	.82	.531	4.11	.98	.694
33	Team spirit	4.16	.96	.650	4.70	.51	.396	3.82	1.02	.691
57	True feeling	4.08	.97	.614	4.27	.79	.458	3.95	1.09	.641
25	Intuitive	4.16	.92	.608	4.27	.97	.503	4.00	.92	.649
73	Visit ailing	3.97	1.10	.590	3.93	1.00	.636	3.91	1.20	.599
69	Diversity	3.84	1.00	.573	3.95	.94	.386	3.77	1.03	.637
97	Politics	4.31	.86	.545	4.41	.66	.506	4.23	.96	.548
93	Shares lead.	4.21	.86	.500	4.20	.95	.182	4.16	.85	.663
77	Visits units	3.61	.95	.498	3.98	.79	.379	3.38	1.01	.492
37	Rides along	2.95	1.35	.476	3.36	1.18	.508	2.61	1.38	.428
65	Sends cards	3.54	1.29	.463	3.95	.96	.588	3.30	1.39	.395
45	Uniform	3.46	1.46	.461	3.93	1.25	.281	3.22	1.53	.481
89	Meets retiring	3.87	1.18	.449	4.02	1.05	.558	3.71	1.28.	.400
9	Greets hirees	3.55	1.34	.434	3.70	1.21	.331	3.44	1.38	.459
21	Meets leaders	4.29	.84	.421	4.32	.64	.540	4.24	.94	.393
29	Families	4.50	.82	.418	4.66	.68	.324	4.38	.91	.419
61	Committee mtgs.	4.16	.93	.416	4.00	.84	.346	4.23	1.00	.499
1	Criticism	3.98	.98	.403	3.93	.95	.267	3.91	1.03	.466
85	Risk taking	3.32	1.19	.399	3.43	1.28	.295	3.21	1.13	.444
5	Citizen input	3.96	1.02	.386	3.82	.95	.394	3.93	1.07	.418
13	Add's academy	4.54	.91	.374	4.45	.93	.570	4.56	.93	.344
17	Delegates	3.62	1.30	.153	3.48	1.25	.117	3.61	1.37	.188

Note: Combined total 25-item scale scores: Mean: 3.95   S.D.: .56

Note in *Table A-3* that Item 37 (rides along with patrol officers from time to time) produced, at 2.95, the only mean on the leader scale below the neutral midpoint of 3.0. However, it also generated a 1.35 standard deviation, indicating considerable disagreement among the respondents. Note also that Item

45 (wears the agency's uniform periodically) produced the highest standard deviation of all the items in the leader scale.

Of particular theoretical importance to this research, Item 17 (delegates day-to-day responsibility for management of the agency to a trusted subordinate) produced a very low item-to-total correlation within both populations. For the chiefs the figure was .117; for assistants, .188. Item 93 (shares responsibility for organizational leadership), on the other hand, reveals a dramatically large difference in item-to-total correlations between chiefs (.182) and assistants (.663). Both items deal with sharing and delegating responsibility. Apparently, the chiefs do not see either item as a leadership function, but the assistants draw a large distinction between the more general "sharing" of responsibility versus the specific "delegation" of responsibility.

Table A-4 reveals three items that produced substantial differences in item-to-total correlations between the chiefs and the assistants on the leader-manager scale. Item 10 (works to develop leadership capabilities throughout the supervisory ranks) exhibits a .272 correlation within the chiefs' population and a .711 correlation among the assistants. For Item 38 (ensures the health, safety, and well-being of the work force), the correlations are .324 and .716 for the chiefs and the assistants, respectively. Item 82 (goes to the scene of all officer-involved shootings that result in death) produced a .061 correlation for the chiefs and a .367 correlation for the assistants.

The comparatively lower standard deviations for the items composing the leader-manager scale indicate a high degree of consensus among the respondents on these particular variables.

The manager-leader scale (*Table A-5*) also produced three items that exhibit low item-to-total correlations among the chiefs but at least moderately robust correlations within the assistants' population. The correlation for chiefs on Item 35 (sets standards of performance and conduct for all personnel)

Table A-4

Correlations of Items to Other Items Within the Leader-Manager Scale of the PLPS

Item	Description	Total (N=144)			Chiefs (N=52)			Assistants (N=92)		
		Mean	S.D.	Item-to-Total Corr.	Mean	S.D.	Item-to-Total Corr.	Mean	S.D.	Item-to-Total Corr.
86	Initiative	4.30	.90	.837	4.57	.55	.665	4.07	1.03	.850
50	Communication	4.11	.93	.812	4.55	.59	.619	3.85	1.02	.818
42	Feedback	4.25	1.01	.795	4.59	.58	.605	4.05	1.06	.804
18	Responsibility	4.40	.81	.765	4.77	.48	.608	4.15	.88	.754
54	Practices	4.50	.78	.754	4.68	.52	.690	4.33	.89	.751
14	Expectations	4.33	.82	.754	4.68	.52	.634	4.09	.89	.739
90	New ideas	4.40	.86	.716	4.68	.56	.653	4.20	.97	.697
66	Hospitable	4.06	.99	.706	4.25	.81	.644	3.88	1.06	.716
6	Challenges	4.44	.72	.703	4.50	.63	.529	4.23	.79	.691
10	Develops	4.34	.88	.697	4.77	.42	.272	4.07	.95	.711
2	Facilitates	4.37	.77	.673	4.57	.63	.507	4.21	.83	.690
38	Health/safety	4.22	.85	.658	4.50	.76	.324	4.01	.88	.716
70	Promoter	4.64	.60	.653	4.66	.53	.615	4.61	.64	.706
30	Openness	4.69	.66	.652	4.89	.39	.478	4.52	.76	.644
34	"Open door"	4.22	.93	.616	4.32	.77	.479	4.15	1.03	.664
26	Supp. objectives	4.40	.81	.579	4.75	.44	.563	4.16	.92	.523
46	Safety equip.	3.85	.94	.566	4.05	.86	.429	3.72	.97	.594
74	Honest	4.61	.76	.560	4.73	.54	.460	4.55	.86	.577
62	Corrects	4.13	.99	.558	4.41	.82	.412	4.00	.97	.568
78	Supervises mtgs.	3.64	1.00	.549	4.02	.79	.554	3.41	1.10	.497
22	Open to commun.	4.41	.80	.524	4.50	.63	.525	4.32	.89	.523
58	Nondiscriminatory	4.60	.68	.520	4.70	.55	.588	4.55	.74	.506
98	Rides w/detectives	2.62	1.22	.357	3.02	1.17	.294	2.37	1.01	.314
94	Meets chiefs	4.20	.94	.330	4.27	.79	.222	4.16	1.01	.358
82	Officer shootings	4.00	1.33	.274	3.95	1.28	.061	3.99	1.40	.367

Note: Combined total 25-item scale scores: Mean: 4.20   S.D.: .57

is .184; for assistants, .583. For Item 31 (ensures that all agency personnel are given relevant education and training), the correlations for chiefs and assistants are .235 and .520, respectively; for Item 19 (communicates clear expectations for professional conduct of all employees), the figures are .153 and .443, respectively.

Table A-5

Correlations of Items to Other Items Within the Manager-Leader Scale of the PLPS

Item	Description	Total (N=144)			Chiefs (N=52)			Assistants (N=92)		
		Mean	S.D.	Item-to-Total Corr.	Mean	S.D.	Item-to-Total Corr.	Mean	S.D.	Item-to-Total Corr.
63	Specific objectives	3.49	1.16	.675	3.50	1.11	.600	3.49	1.18	.714
67	Case cancellations	2.80	1.08	.668	3.05	1.10	.768	2.63	1.08	.622
47	Mission	4.37	.85	.642	4.68	.56	.377	4.17	.93	.728
43	Knows	3.80	1.01	.636	3.80	1.11	.724	3.83	.98	.614
71	Evaluates	4.26	.91	.615	4.48	.66	.515	4.09	1.02	.644
55	Vehicle fleet	3.66	1.03	.603	3.75	1.01	.548	3.60	1.09	.624
27	Planning	4.13	.82	.589	4.23	.77	.626	4.05	.83	.568
87	Policies	4.19	.89	.518	4.05	1.01	.551	4.22	.85	.539
11	Priorities	4.07	1.03	.510	3.93	1.15	.304	4.17	.93	.673
39	Per capita	3.32	1.01	.493	3.18	.95	.621	3.39	1.02	.468
79	Chain of command	3.49	1.16	.486	3.59	1.21	.461	3.40	1.20	.493
3	Mgmt. theory	4.39	.70	.481	4.43	.70	.452	4.37	.73	.492
35	Perform./conduct	4.33	.85	.473	4.48	.79	.184	4.20	.87	.583
51	Span of cont.	4.11	.90	.470	4.34	.75	.417	3.99	.95	.478
23	Inspects personnel	3.13	1.28	.463	3.45	1.15	.339	2.90	1.29	.502
59	Monitors radio	3.72	1.09	.459	3.77	1.05	.542	3.68	1.14	.424
99	Research	3.58	1.03	.457	3.75	.84	.370	3.41	1.12	.477
31	Training	4.39	.78	.456	4.75	.49	.235	4.18	.82	.520
75	Directs work	3.54	1.05	.445	3.52	1.09	.459	3.56	1.08	.449
91	Work flow	2.90	1.07	.427	2.86	1.05	.443	2.84	1.11	.423
83	Mgmt. rights	4.19	.86	.402	4.02	.85	.467	4.33	.82	.423
19	Professional	4.56	.78	.390	4.91	.29	.153	4.32	.91	.443
95	Resources	4.08	.89	.382	4.05	.86	.581	4.07	.91	.307
15	Runs mtgs.	3.91	1.00	.354	3.34	.86	.564	4.28	.91	.443
7	Inspects offices	3.44	1.06	.341	3.70	1.00	.193	3.29	1.05	.389

Note: Combined total 25-item scale scores: Mean: 3.82 S.D.: .53

The manager scale *(Table A-6)* produced two item-to-total correlations worthy of note. First, Item 44 (has an aide represent him or her at most ceremonial functions) is noteworthy because it is the only item in the PLPS that exhibits the lowest item-to-total correlation. Second, Item 92 (cultivates an attitude that he or she is the person most responsible for how things are going in the agency) is significant because the chiefs' item-to-total correlation is, unlike most other items in the PLPS, substantially *higher* than the assistants'.

Table A-6
Correlations of Items to Other Items Within the Manager Scale of the PLPS

Item	Description	Total (N=144)			Chiefs (N=52)			Assistants (N=92)		
		Mean	S.D.	Item-to-Total Corr.	Mean	S.D.	Item-to-Total Corr.	Mean	S.D.	Item-to-Total Corr.
80	"Detail"	3.42	1.20	.747	3.16	1.12	.728	3.57	1.26	.748
36	Organizer	3.86	.90	.666	3.91	.86	.731	3.85	.94	.657
24	Law	3.70	1.01	.639	3.57	1.02	.638	3.71	1.06	.639
64	Computer	3.11	.94	.606	2.95	.81	.695	3.12	1.00	.567
68	Technical	2.67	1.21	.601	2.32	1.16	.517	2.85	1.21	.626
28	Boss's Q's	4.14	.89	.592	3.75	.97	.642	4.37	.79	.551
16	Control	3.98	.97	.589	3.75	1.01	.698	4.15	.93	.511
72	Logical	4.00	.95	.580	3.89	.97	.668	4.04	.96	.529
56	Output	3.32	1.09	.580	3.48	.95	.565	3.17	1.17	.647
12	Problem	3.40	1.12	.571	3.27	1.11	.553	3.49	1.07	.572
60	Signs off.	2.95	1.24	.563	2.95	1.12	.605	3.00	1.31	.554
84	Technical Ques.	3.35	1.13	.562	2.82	.97	.607	3.68	1.06	.532
96	Authority	4.00	.92	.534	4.14	.88	.465	3.90	.94	.619
76	Manage	3.75	1.00	.523	3.36	1.04	.501	3.93	.97	.511
32	Budget	4.20	.85	.512	4.16	.78	.484	4.22	.92	.529
20	Office	3.79	1.14	.458	3.16	1.18	.652	4.12	.99	.323
48	Coordination	3.41	1.02	.454	3.20	.88	.466	3.54	1.10	.434
100	Overtime	3.02	1.11	.431	3.14	1.07	.416	2.94	1.17	.472
81	Analytic	3.72	.99	.429	4.16	.78	.366	3.79	.98	.454
40	Nonroutine	3.35	1.22	.405	3.25	1.10	.465	3.44	1.31	.372
52	Neutral	3.94	1.04	.349	4.14	.93	.374	3.78	1.11	.396
4	Budget	4.11	.96	.321	4.18	.95	.446	4.06	1.00	.282
92	Most responsible	3.61	1.27	.256	3.39	1.20	.456	3.68	1.28	.140
88	"Buy money"	2.13	1.21	.230	2.11	1.04	.247	2.16	1.27	.224
44	Ceremonial	2.42	1.20	.054	2.52	1.07	.102	2.44	1.28	.132

Note: Combined total 25-item scale scores: Mean: 3.50   S.D.: .57

It is significant that of the 100 items on the PLPS, only 8 produced combined mean scores below the 3.0 midpoint (the combined means average 3.87). This is important because it provides support for the finding that little distinction between leadership functions and management functions is apparently being made by big-city police leaders in the United States.

Frequency Distributions

After the reliability analysis was completed, attention was turned to the frequency distribution of respondents' answers to survey items in order to discern patterns that might be reflected in the distribution of responses.

Tables A-3–A-6 offer one way of looking at the distribution of PLPS scores by scale. The histogram offers, in graphic form, a much clearer indication of how the respondents scored on the PLPS. It allows for a quick and direct examination of the shape, variability, and item concentrations of survey responses.

Figures A-1–A-8 are histograms that include not only the "picture" of the respondents' scores but also the mean, median, standard deviation, kurtosis, skewness, range, and minimum and maximum scores for each of the four scales. The SPSS^x program also superimposes over the histogram the classic "bell-shaped" curve of the type most commonly associated with theoretically normal distributions. Periods are used to indicate the distribution of cases had there been a normal distribution (with the same mean and variance). To facilitate comparisons, the histograms for each scale will be presented first for the chiefs, then for the assistants.

As seen in *Figures A-1* and *A-2*, the chiefs' and assistants' responses do not reveal a parallel pattern for the leader scale, especially as evidenced by the significantly higher mean scores of the chiefs (4.71 versus 3.88 for the assistants).

Figure A-1
Frequency Distribution of the Leader Scale of
the PLPS: Chiefs Only
(N=52)

Count Midpoint   (One symbol equals approximately .21 occurrences)

```
0    3.0    .
0    3.1    .
1    3.2    *·***
1    3.3    **·**
0    3.4    .
2    3.5    ******·***
3    3.6    *********·*****
3    3.7    ************·*
5    3.8    ****************·********
3    3.9    *************      .
3    4.0    *************        .
1    4.1    *****               .
4    4.2    ******************   .
3    4.3    *************       .
6    4.4    ***********************·********
4    4.5    ****************·**
9    4.6    ************·*****************************
2    4.7    **********.
0    4.8         .
2    4.9    ****·*****
0    5.0         .
           I .... +.... I .... + .... I .... + .... I.... + .... I .... + .... I
           0       4       8      12      16      20
                              Percent
```

Mean	4.71	Median	4.26	S.D.	.43
Kurtosis	-.77	Skewness	-.4272	Range	1.72
Minimum	3.16	Maximum	4.88		

A-22

Figure A-2
Frequency Distribution of the Leader Scale of
the PLPS: Assistants Only
(N=92)

Count	Midpoint	(One symbol equals approximately .36 occurrences)
1	1.90	***
1	2.05	***
0	2.20	.
0	2.35	.
0	2.50	.
2	2.65	**·**
1	2.80	*** .
3	2.95	*******·
4	3.10	**********·
6	3.25	*************·**
2	3.40	*****
4	3.55	**********
14	3.70	******************************·*************
7	3.85	******************
9	4.00	************************·*
8	4.15	********************·
7	4.30	*****************·
11	4.45	****************·*************
6	4.60	*************·****
3	4.75	********·
2	4.90	*****.

```
          I .... + .... I .... + .... I .... + .... I .... + .... I .... + .... I
          0        4        8        12       16       20
                                  Percent
```

Mean	3.88	Median	3.96	S.D.	.60
Kurtosis	.50	Skewness	-.74	Range	2.92
Minimum	1.96	Maximum	4.88		

Figure A-3
Frequency Distribution of the Leader-Manager Scale of the PLPS: Chiefs Only (N=52)

Count Midpoint   (One symbol equals approximately .16 occurrences)

```
0   3.550  .
1   3.625  :*****
1   3.700  *:****
1   3.775  **:***
1   3.850  ****:*
0   3.925
1   4.000  ******
2   4.075  ************.
3   4.150  *****************.*
2   4.225  ************
3   4.300  ******************
3   4.375  *****************
4   4.450  *************************
5   4.525  *****************************.**
4   4.600  *************************
7   4.675  ********************************.********************
4   4.750  **********************.****
2   4.825  ************
5   4.900  *************.****************
3   4.975  **************.********
0   5.050       .
           I .... + .... I .... + .... I .... + .... I ....+ .... I .... + .... I
           0         3          6          9         12         15
                                    Percent
```

Mean	4.94	Median	4.56	S.D.	.34
Kurtosis	.06	Skewness	-.74	Range	1.36
Minimum	3.64	Maximum	5.00		

As with the leader scale, the leader-manager scale (*Figures A-3* and *A-4*) reflects important differences in the response pattern of the chiefs and the assistants. Again, the most prominent difference may be found in the mean scores (4.94 for the chiefs, 4.08 for the assistants).

Figure A-4

Frequency Distribution of the Leader-Manager Scale of the PLPS: Assistants Only (N=92)

Count Midpoint   (One symbol equals approximately .27 occurrences)

Count	Midpoint	
0	2.15	
2	2.30	:******
1	2.45	:***
1	2.60	*:**
0	2.75	.
1	2.90	****.
2	3.05	*******.
4	3.20	***********·***
1	3.35	****
9	3.50	***********************·***********
5	3.65	*****************
2	3.80	*******
6	3.95	********************
10	4.10	********************************·*****
10	4.25	********************************·******
9	4.40	****************************·*****
10	4.55	***************************·***********
9	4.70	***********************·*************
4	4.85	**************·.
5	5.00	***********·*******
0	5.15	.

```
I ....+ .... I ....+ .... I ....+ .... I ....+ .... I ....+ .... I
0        3        6        9        12       15
                    Percent
```

Mean	4.08	Median	4.20	S.D.	.62
Kurtosis	.41	Skewness	-.85	Range	2.72
Minimum	2.28	Maximum	5.00		

Figure A-5
Frequency Distribution of the Manager-Leader Scale of the PLPS: Chiefs Only
(N=52)

Count	Midpoint	(One symbol equals approximately .21 occurrences)
0	2.30	
0	2.45	
0	2.60	.
1	2.75	:****
1	2.90	**·**
1	3.05	*****.
1	3.20	*****
4	3.35	***************·****
2	3.50	**********
7	3.65	*****************************·******
8	3.80	*********************************·******
6	3.95	***************************
6	4.10	***************************.
5	4.25	***********************.
4	4.40	*****************·*
3	4.55	************·**
1	4.70	*****
2	4.85	***·******
0	5.00	.
0	5.15	.
0	5.30	

```
I .... + .... I .... + .... I .... + .... I .... + .... I .... + .... I
0          4          8         12         16         20
                          Percent
```

Mean	3.91	Median	3.88	S.D.	.46
Kurtosis	-.07	Skewness	-.17	Range	2.12
Minimum	2.76	Maximum	4.88		

While mean scores of the two respondent groups are very close, the steep kurtosis seen in *Figures A-5* and *A-6* underscores the lack of a common pattern in chief and assistant responses to the manager-leader scale.

Figure A-6

Frequency Distribution of the Manager-Leader Scale of the PLPS: Assistants Only
(N=92)

Count Midpoint (One symbol equals approximately .36 occurrences)

Count	Midpoint	
0	1.80	
1	1.95	***
0	2.10	
0	2.25	.
0	2.40	.
2	2.55	*·***
1	2.70	***.
3	2.85	******·*
6	3.00	**********·******
4	3.15	********** .
4	3.30	********** .
4	3.45	********** .
9	3.60	**********************·.
8	3.75	******************** .
8	3.90	******************** .
14	4.05	**************************·*************
8	4.20	******************·**
8	4.35	******************·******
5	4.50	***********·**
6	4.65	*******·********
0	4.80	.

```
I .... + .... I .... + .... I .... + .... I .... + .... I .... + .... I
0        4        8        12        16        20
                        Percent
```

Mean	3.79	Median	3.88	S.D.	.57
Kurtosis	.14	Skewness	-.67	Range	2.72
Minimum	1.96	Maximum	4.68		

The histograms for the manager scale (*Figures A-7* and *A-8*) show clearly that skewness in responses for the two groups is in opposite directions. While both chiefs and assistants tend to attach lesser significance to the management functions, the

Figure A-7
Frequency Distribution of the Manager Scale
of the PLPS: Chiefs Only
(N=52)

Count	Midpoint	(One symbol equals approximately .16 occurrences)
1	2.4	****.*
1	2.5	******
2	2.6	********.****
2	2.7	**********.*
6	2.8	*****************.**********************
3	2.9	****************.**
3	3.0	*****************.
2	3.1	************
6	3.2	**********************.**************
2	3.3	************
5	3.4	*************************.********
2	3.5	*************
1	3.6	******
3	3.7	******************.
2	3.8	*************
1	3.9	******
2	4.0	***********.*
2	4.1	********.****
3	4.2	*******.************
1	4.3	****.*
2	4.4	***.*********

```
I .... + .... I .... + .... I .... + .... I .... + .... I .... + .... I
0          3          6          9          12          15
                          Percent
```

Mean	3.35	Median	3.26	S.D.	.55
Kurtosis	-.84	Skewness	.31	Range	2.08
Minimum	2.36	Maximum	4.44		

assistants as a group apparently view their superiors as much more involved in distinctly managerial work than the chiefs seem to believe is appropriate.

Figure A-8
Frequency Distribution of the Manager Scale of the PLPS: Assistants Only
(N=92)

Count	Midpoint	(One symbol equals approximately .36 occurrences)
1	1.65	***
0	1.80	
0	1.95	
0	2.10	.
0	2.25	.
1	2.40	**:
5	2.55	****·*********
2	2.70	***** .
2	2.85	***** .
3	3.00	******** .
8	3.15	******************·**
9	3.30	*********************·**
10	3.45	***********************·*
7	3.60	******************
6	3.75	**************** .
14	3.90	*********************·***************
10	4.05	***********************·********
5	4.20	*************·.
2	4.35	***** .
5	4.50	******·*******
1	4.65	***.

```
      I ....+ ....I ....+ ....I ....+ ....I ....+ ....I ....+ ....I ....+ ....I
      0       4        8       12       16       20
                            Percent
```

Mean	3.58	Median	3.56	S.D.	.57
Kurtosis	.37	Skewness	-.56	Range	2.92
Minimum	1.68	Maximum	4.60		

Intercorrelations Among the Four PLPS Scales

Posited at the beginning of this research was the idea of a leadership-management continuum along which police executive functions could be discerned. This section puts to the test that idea.

A "4 x 4" table. The PLPS consists of four scales: leader, leader-manager, manager-leader, and manager. A convenient way of presenting the intercorrelations among the four scales is through the use of a "4 x 4" table. Use of Pearson correlation coefficients reveals that each of the scales is correlated against the others. If the suggestion that gradients of police leadership and management functions can be distinguished on a continuum is confirmed, a trend to that effect will have emerged in the data. Such is the case with the PLPS, as observed in *Table A-7*.

Table A-7

Pearson Correlation Coefficients for the Four Scales of the PLPS (N=143)

	LEADER	LEADER-MANAGER	MANAGER-LEADER	MANAGER
LEADER				
LEADER-MANAGER	.897 p=.000			
MANAGER-LEADER	.698 p=.000	.753 p=.000		
MANAGER	.484 p=.000	.515 p=.000	.828 p=.000	

Made clear in *Table A-7* are two important findings. First, the theoretical construct of the leader-through-manager scales of the PLPS has been found to be empirically validated. In other words, the intercorrelations among the four scales are precisely as predicted: the leader scale correlates best with the leader-manager scale, then with the manager-leader scale. It correlates most weakly with the manager scale. Second, the possibility that these correlations might have been produced by chance is less than one in a thousand.

It is instructive to note once again, however, that the .484 correlation between the two poles of the continuum (leader versus manager) is quite high. This indicates that PLPS respondents, while evidencing some degree of value discrimination between leadership and management functions, seem to suggest that virtually all of those executive functions are of great importance to police administration and the direct responsibility of the police chief executive.

Factor analysis. Evidence of reliability—Cronbach's alphas for the four scales and item-to-total correlations within each scale—has been established empirically for the PLPS, as has evidence of posited intercorrelations among the four scales. Attention is now turned to a factor analysis of the variables of the survey instrument.

The factor analysis permits a view of the actual logic of the subjects' responses to the survey items. By use of $SPSS^x$, each of the 100 variables was correlated against the other 99. Factor analysis of this huge amount of data (literally 10,000 possible correlations) shows how well or how poorly each variable "loads" with other clustered variables both within and beyond its own scale. By means of the factor analysis, survey items that may have been inappropriately classified according to the theoretical model of leader-through-manager, or that may have been "bad" items (for example, confusing or ambiguous language, or the use of two conditions in a single item), can be identified and, if desired, eliminated. Furthermore, a factor analysis provides a confirmatory empirical test (based on the observed patterns of responses in the data set) of the theoretical logic that led to the construction of the original four scales of the PLPS.

The principal purpose of the elimination of items from a scale is to render the scale more parsimonious, to make it as clear and as economical an indicator of what is being measured as possible. On this basis, and guided by a rotated principal factor analysis using the VARIMAX method, it was decided to "eliminate" for purposes of further analysis 35 of the items from the PLPS. That simplifying procedure, in turn, led to a conclusion that only the poles of the original leader-through-manager continuum were needed as a framework for the additional analysis. In effect, the two middle gradients—leader-manager and manager-leader—were factored out of the model as their respective variables clustered parsimoniously with either the leader or the manager dimensions. This is not meant to imply that the original four-scale model is without value. On the contrary, its practical implications are believed (and have been shown above) to be quite significant. Further, with modifications to the research design, it is possible that the original model can be of substantial worth to continuing research in the field of police executive leadership.

Before dispensing with the four-scale model that inspired this research, it should be noted that many of the rejected variables continue to have major theoretical importance to the research at hand. For that reason, they are listed in *Table A-8* and discussed in greater detail later in this appendix.

Table A-8

PLPS Items Dropped From Further Consideration in the Analysis of Responses

Item	Description	Original Scale
3	Knows, understands modern management theory	M-L
7	Personally inspects offices periodically	M-L
8	Is seen as analytical	M
9	Personally greets all new employees	L
17	Delegates day-to-day responsibility to assistant	L
19	Makes clear expectation for professionalism	M-L
23	Inspects uniformed officers from time to time	M-L
31	Ensures that all are given relevant training	M-L
35	Sets standards for performance, conduct for all	M-L
37	Rides along with patrol officers from time to time	L
38	Ensures health, safety, well-being of employees	L-M
40	Reviews all nonroutine expenditures	M
44	Has aide represent at most ceremonial functions	M
46	Ensures that safety equipment is up to date	L-M
47	Defines mission and objectives of agency	M-L
51	Maintains reasonable span of control	M-L
55	Ensures that vehicle fleet is well maintained	M-L
59	Monitors the police radio periodically	M-L
62	Corrects or dismisses poor performers	L-M
64	Thoroughly familiar with computer programs	M
66	Creates a hospitable work environment	L-M
70	Seen as enthusiastic promoter of agency	L-M
71	Evaluates systematically overall performance	M-L
77	Makes frequent visits to units within agency	L
78	Attends supervisors meetings periodically	L-M
82	Goes to scene of officer shootings; death cases	L-M
83	Seen as strong advocate of management rights	M-L
85	Encourages risk taking by employees at all levels	L
88	Responsible for dispensing drug "buy money"	M
89	Personally meets with retiring employees	L
92	Cultivates attitude as one most responsible	M
93	Shares responsibility for agency leadership	L
94	Meets often chiefs of other agencies	L-M
98	Rides along periodically with homicide, vice	L-M
99	Participates in research to increase efficiency	M-L

Leader-34, Manager-31. In any event, a newly evolved 65-item, two-dimension general model of executive leadership (34 items) and management (31 items) has emerged from the research. It represents an intersection of empirically parsimonious results with a more exacting and potentially useful theory of police executive leadership. The results of the rotated factor analysis show two broad dimensions—"Leader-34" and "Manager-31"—that contain four factors and five factors, respectively. *Tables A-9–A-10* present these factors.

Table A-9
Factor Analysis of Leader-34 Items of the PLPS (N=144)

		Factors			
Item	Description	1	2	3	4
10	Develops leadership capabilities	.774			
81	Inspires shared vision of future	.771			
33	Builds team spirit, teamwork	.764			
6	Challenges people to do better	.756			
26	Enlists support in setting objectives	.750			
18	Develops responsibility in subordinates	.736			
14	Makes clear expectations of performance	.734			
86	Encourages initiative throughout agency	.719			
2	Facilitates work of agency employees	.672			
50	Uses all means to communicate	.666			
54	Practices what he or she preaches	.649			
58	Is clear on nondiscrimination policy	.628			
42	Elicits feedback on policies, practices	.608			
57	Shares true feelings about agency issues	.597			
90	Encourages new ideas by all members	.557			
41	Acts as model of expected behavior	.555			
25	Approaches work intuitively, creatively	.554			
97	Masters internal, external politics	.457			
53	Recognizes publicly fine, heroic work	.457			
74	Seen by employees as absolutely honest	.445			
30	Encourages openness, honesty	.423			
49	Celebrates accomplishments of workers	.410			
13	Addresses each new academy class	.410			
73	Visits hospitalized members		.770		
45	Wears the uniform periodically		.712		
65	Sends cards to injured or ill employees		.698		
29	Visits families of slain, injured officers		.643		
21	Meets often with community leaders			.856	
22	Is open to community feedback			.792	
61	Attends many community meetings			.744	
5	Invites citizen input on agency policies			.707	
1	Encourages questioning, criticism				.759
69	Places high value on diversity of opinion				.617
34	Develops, encourages use of "open door"				.505
	% of Variance Explained:	49.5	6.4	4.7	3.6
	Cronbach Alpha for Leader-34: .954				

A-34

Table A-10

Factor Analysis of Manager-31 Items of the PLPS
(N=143)

Item Description		1	2	Factors 3	4	5
67	Sets norms, monitors case cancellations	.697				
91	Responsible for work flow	.682				
56	Sets precise work output standards	.659				
100	Sets limits for, controls overtime	.599				
63	Sets specific objectives for units	.580				
60	Signs off on all correspondence	.576				
48	Coordinates major activities of agency	.473				
11	Personally sets agency priorities		.737			
12	Seen as agency's problem solver		.679			
16	Maintains control at all times		.641			
15	Runs meetings he/she attends		.585			
20	Spends much time in the office		.570			
76	Controls key managerial processes		.447			
75	Personally directs subordinates' work		.431			
84	Able to answer technical questions now			.771		
68	Has more technical expertise			.653		
28	Able to answer boss's questions now			.632		
24	Intimately familiar with the law			.560		
52	Seen as neutral, objective manager				.834	
72	Is logical, orderly, unemotional				.736	
36	Known as effective organizer				.549	
43	Knows at all time what is going on				.473	
80	Seen as good "detail" person				.473	
79	Enforces chain of command				.430	
96	Sets unequivocal lines of authority				.422	
4	Intimately involved in budget					.856
32	Constantly up to date on budget					.620
27	Intimately involved in planning					.504
39	Personally monitors per capita costs					.450
87	Personally works on agency policies					.405
95	Responsible for resource allocation					.405
% of Variance Explained:		35.4	6.3	6.1	5.5	4.1
Cronbach Alpha for Manager-31: .938						

The four-factor Leader-34 scale *(Table A-9)* produces an extremely robust reliability coefficient of .954. Likewise, the five factors of the Manager-31 scale *(Table A-10)* exhibit exceptionally strong internal consistency with an overall reliability coefficient of .938.

The Rejected Items

A re-examination of those items (variables) dropped from the PLPS *(see Table A-8)* as a result of reliability and factor analyses reveals that most, if not all, do have at least some theoretical importance. Several appear to be quite important. Because the principal concern of this study is the quality of police leadership in America, selected examples from the original leader dimension are presented. They are accompanied by the researcher's speculations about their failure to survive the analytical review.

Personally greets all new employees (Item 9). This survey item represents a leadership practice that is considered by many observers (Block, 1987; Schein, 1985; and others) to be an important step in the process of introducing new employees to the organization's values, principles, and expectations. It is an especially valuable opportunity to begin the process of "embedding organizational culture" (Schein, 1985).

First impressions are often lasting impressions, and most police officers remember vividly their first day on the job. The police chief who addresses each new academy class (PLPS Item 13 in Appendix B), for example, can use the occasion to help instill in each new officer a sense of the agency's commitment to effective crime fighting, community service, and professional values and behavior. It is also an excellent opportunity to welcome the new officers and to congratulate them on their success in the selection process.

It is possible that Item 9 had to be rejected because of confusion about the term "personally." Does this mean greeting the new employees "individually?" If so, the logistical problems, especially in the larger agencies, may have seemed to the chiefs to be insurmountable. This would be particularly true of those chiefs whose managerial orientations keep them fully occupied. Another explanation, of course, is that while the chiefs attach significance to the function (4.50 mean), it simply does not load well with other "culture-embedding" functions.

Nonetheless, rejection of this item begins to suggest that the chiefs may not be taking full advantage of a pivotal opportunity to help shape the views and opinions and, consequently, the future behavior of their new officers.

Delegates day-to-day responsibility for management of the agency to a trusted subordinate (Item 17). This item was designated a leader dimension because, perhaps more than any other variable, it underscores the practical as well as the theoretical difference between executive leadership and executive management. There is a strong indication that unless today's police chiefs delegate their managerial responsibilities to trusted others, their leadership roles cannot be fulfilled to maximum potential.

There is reason to speculate that many of the respondents, both chiefs and their assistants, see day-to-day managerial duties as the responsibility of the chief executive. Even when a chief executive may in actual practice delegate the managerial function to an immediate subordinate, it is possible that the chief feels that he or she ought not to do so, that there is something wrong with delegating such a large responsibility. Also, a strong likelihood exists that the two terms, *leadership* and *management,* are viewed and used synonymously by police chiefs. Certainly, the vast body of literature (see Chapter Two) fails to take into account any theoretical or practical distinction between the two functions.

The "management" of the police organization has traditionally been the job of the police chief; responses to this item (and especially its 1.30 standard deviation[*]) suggest that ambivalence toward that tradition may be growing.

Rides along with patrol officers from time to time (Item 37). Another of the "culture embedding" or "culture management" variables, this item is consistent with the literature

---

[*]The standard deviation measures the average dispersion of variables' values about their mean. The larger the standard deviation, the less closely grouped about the mean are the values of the variables.

(Bennis and Nanus, 1985; Peters, 1984; Peters and Waterman, 1982) that argues that leaders must engage the work force. That is, they must spend time—and considerable amounts of it—interacting with the people who have been hired to do the primary work of the organization. By this means, it is suggested, leaders show their support and concern for the workers, and they receive important feedback on organizational effectiveness, efficiency, and morale.

There appears to be a great deal of ambivalence about the value—or perhaps the propriety—of police chiefs riding along from time to time with their officers. This may be the result of the respondents' belief that it is generally impermissible to "violate" the chain of command by communicating directly with the officers, bypassing intermediate supervisors and managers. The ambivalence may also result from a belief of some that it is simply not "appropriate" for the agency's top administrator to spend time on an activity whose purpose is subject to misinterpretations. This may be especially true given the paramilitary bureaucratic structure and orientation of policing, which tend to breed mistrust and suspicion.

Makes frequent visits to units throughout the organization (Item 77). Based on the same rationale as that cited above, the executive practice of frequent, informal visits to the agency's operational units can have the effect of demonstrating that the administration wants to stay in touch with employee views and concerns.

The respondents' mixed reactions to this item may reflect a belief that the chief executives have others to whom they may turn for such organizational "sensing." That activity, along with others previously discussed, may be seen as extraneous, something the police chiefs can and should do in their spare time.

Encourages risk taking by employees at all levels (Item 85). Much of the literature (Bennis and Nanus, 1985; Block,

1987; Kouzes and Posner, 1987; Peters and Waterman, 1982) suggests that today's organizations need to encourage risk-taking behavior by employees at all levels. It is through such behavior that innovative programs are developed and that creative solutions are brought to bear on organizational problems and challenges.

Perhaps the confusion or concern implied in the respondents' reactions to this item is based on the absence of a qualifier for the term "risk taking." Risks may, for example, be seen as wise risks or reckless risks. It is possible that, while law enforcement executives may accept the theoretical value of organizational risk taking, some of the respondents to this survey may have erred on the side of caution, believing that policing has no room for carelessness or recklessness.

Personally meets with employees who are retiring (Item 89). This item might have relied for its theoretical relevance on the long-established value of exit interviews as a means of capturing important information on organizational conditions. However, its use in the PLPS was predicated on a belief that the practice of meeting with employees who are retiring is also an effective "culture management" activity. It represents another means by which chief executives communicate their interest in their personnel.

Given the two rationales for inclusion of this item—that of gaining information vis-à-vis that of symbolizing interest—it is clear why confusion may have existed among the respondents.

Shares responsibility for organizational leadership (Item 93). Relying on Bradford and Cohen's well-developed argument for shared responsibility of organizational leadership, this item has a vital theoretical foundation. Effective leadership is needed at all levels of agency activity. Indeed, the police executive leader cannot hope to be successful, for example, in the absence of competent leadership at the sergeants' position. On a practical level, "subordinates must interact with one another—consulting, checking, cajoling and confronting—without always going through the boss" (1984: 170).

It is possible that some PLPS respondents associate shared responsibility with the structure of committees, task forces, and other arrangements that have, in their experience, produced unnecessary time delays and other negative outcomes.

If— as is strongly argued by Bennis and Nanus (1985), Peters and Waterman (1982), Burns (1978), and others— there is an important difference between the organizational functions of leadership and management, the PLPS offers the police world a means of identifying those differences. It also provides an opportunity for police executives to assess the extent to which they have operationalized—in the structures of their organizations and in their own practices—the distinction between leadership and management.

Demographic Correlates

This section presents correlations between the demographic characteristics of the chiefs' subsample only and the chiefs' responses to the PLPS. While statistical significance is scant, some clear trends in the data emerged. To assess those trends it is necessary to resurrect at least momentarily the original four scales of the leader-through-manager model. That will permit a more detailed examination of the demographic characteristics.

Attention will be focused both on individual respondent variables (education, age, time in policing, time as chief executive) and on contextual variables (size of city, size of agency).

Table A-11

Pearson Correlations Between Respondent Demographic Characteristics and Scores on Six of the PLPS Scales (Chiefs Only) (N=52)

	Education	Age	Time in Policing	Time as Chief
Leader	-.079	-.104	-.325*	-.190
Leader-Manager	-.162	.082	-.118	-.124
Manager-Leader	-.260	.129	-.041	.023
Manager	-.384*	.123	.012	.064
Leader-34	-.139	-.036	-.211	-.109
Manager-31	-.342*	.148	.044	.105

*Significant at p<.01

Education. *Table A-11*, which presents Pearson correlation coefficients* for the four scales of the original model plus the Leader-34 and Manager-31 scales, reveals that the less educated chiefs tend to be increasingly more managerial in their orientation, with both the manager and the Manager-31 scales achieving significance at the .01 level. This trend is clearly linear. Of the specific items, three were negatively correlated to education at the .01 level: Item 15 (runs meetings he or she attends), which produced a .38 F-ratio within the Manager-31 scale; Item 32 (constantly up to date on the budget), part of the

---

*The correlation coefficient measures the linear relationship between two variables, such as between the chiefs' score on the Leader-34 scale and time in policing. The closer the coefficient is to zero, the less likely a linear relationship; the closer to positive one, the more likely that an increase in one variable is associated with an increase in the other; the closer to negative one, the more likely that an increase in one is associated with a decrease in the value of the other.

Manager-31 scale; and Item 76 (controls key managerial processes), also a part of the Manager-31 scale. Finally, Item 40 (reviews all nonroutine expenditures) was significant at the .001 level. This item, part of the original manager scale, was one that had been "eliminated," the result of reliability and factor analyses.

Age. There were no statistically significant correlations between the ages of the chiefs and their responses to the PLPS. However, as seen in *Table A-11*, the findings indicate generally that the younger chiefs are more likely than their older colleagues to profess values most closely associated with the leadership functions. Of the original 100 survey items, only Item 25 (approaches work intuitively; creatively) achieved statistical significance, with a correlation of .356.

Time in policing. Those chiefs with the least amount of time in police work (who are also younger in age) are those who scored the highest in the leadership arena. Generally, time in policing correlated significantly with the leader scale. Four specific survey items also produced a significant correlation against total time in police work, each of which supports the general finding that those chiefs who have the shortest tenure in the profession scored highest on the Leader-34 or the leader scales. Those with the most time in the field scored highest on the managerial scales.

Item 22 (is open to community feedback) correlates against time in policing at -.348; Item 25 (approaches work intuitively, creatively) correlates at -.338; Item 81 (inspires shared vision of future) also correlates at -.338; and Item 98 (rides along from time to time with homicide, vice, narcotics, others), dropped from the original leader-manager scale, correlates against time in policing at -.332.

Time as chief. Another clear trend in the data is that those chiefs who have been in the executive office the shortest period of time (who, again, are also younger) are more likely than their older counterparts to favor leadership functions in the PLPS. Put differently, the longer a chief has been in office the more likely he or she is to embrace the managerial side of police administration.

Two of the survey items achieved significance in the correlation between responses to the PLPS and time as chief. They are Item 53 (recognizes publicly fine, heroic work) at -.348 and Item 78 (attends supervisors meetings from time to time), dropped from the leader-manager scale, at -.343.

Table A-12 presents the findings of correlations between city and agency size and the chiefs' responses to the PLPS. While there are no statistically significant correlations, one finding is clear: generally, the smaller the city and the smaller the agency the more likely it is that the chief will favor the leadership variables of the survey. This does not mean that the chiefs of the smallest of the big-city police departments have necessarily achieved greater congruence between professed values and observed behavior than their counterparts in the larger agencies.

Table A-12

Pearson Correlations Between Contextual Characteristics and Scores on Six of the PLPS Scales (Chiefs Only) (N=52)

	City Rank*	Square Miles	No. Sworn Personnel
Leader	.004	.133	-.052
Leader-Manager	-.106	.093	.178
Manager-Leader	-.149	.131	.129
Manager	-.189	.041	.152
Leader-34	-.132	.167	.126
Manager-31	-.220	.080	.165

*"City Rank," as the title suggests, refers to the population ranking of a given city; the smaller the ranking, the larger the city's population.

City rank. The correlations between city rank and leadership-to-management values exhibit a clearly linear trend: the bigger the city, the more managerial the orientation of the police chief tends to be. There were four significant negative correlations between the population size of a city and the PLPS responses of the chiefs. Item 5 (invites citizen input on agency policies), from the Leader-34 scale, produced a correlation of -.411. Item 11 (personally sets agency priorities), from the Manager-31 scale, produced a correlation of -.380. Item 38 (ensures health, safety, well-being of employees), dropped from the leader-manager scale, correlated at -.334. Item 56 (sets precise work output standards) produced a correlation between rank of city and chiefs' responses of -.339. In addition, there was one positive correlation between city rank and the chiefs' responses; Item 78 (attends supervisors meetings from time to time), dropped from the leader-manager scale, produced a correlation of .350.

Square miles. There were no statistically significant correlations between the number of square miles of the cities and the chiefs' responses to the PLPS. However, several specific items produced correlations that approached significance.

Number of sworn personnel. The survey found that chiefs of smaller agencies are generally more likely to favor the leadership variables of the PLPS, although no significant correlations were produced at the scale level; nor were clearly linear trends discernible. There were, however, three specific survey items that produced significant correlations. Item 9 (personally greets new employees), dropped from the leader scale, correlated negatively at -.339. Item 11 (personally sets agency priorities) correlated at .341. Item 17 (delegates day-to-day responsibility for management to trusted subordinate) produced another negative correlation, this one at -.337.

Summary of demographic and contextual correlates. An analysis of the demographic and contextual correlations thus reveals that those chiefs who are more likely to be inclined than others toward police leadership functions as measured by the survey are more highly educated, are younger, have been in police work less time, have less tenure as chiefs, head agencies in the smallest of the large cities (in population only, not in square miles), and run agencies with fewer sworn personnel.

Research Methodology and Instrumentation: Conclusions

One of the first challenges in deciding how most effectively to gain answers to the four research questions was that of *access*. How can one efficiently obtain accurate information from and about American police chiefs on their leadership practices?

The Survey Approach

The decision to survey the chiefs and their assistants was made because of the likelihood of producing a population large enough to sustain key findings. The opinions and observations of 52 chiefs and 92 assistants, representing 55 cities and 28 states, were obtained. This supports the conclusion that the study, limited though it may be by the restrictions inherent in survey research, offers an important source of valuable information about the thinking and behavior of those who direct and influence police practices in America's large urban centers.

Alternative approaches, considered at length before being rejected because of time constraints, included (1) ethnographic research, which likely would have yielded a rich collection of firsthand observations about the leadership practices of one police chief or a few chiefs; (2) a larger but still limited number of interviews with both chiefs and their assistants; and (3) a combination of direct observations, interviews, and surveying.

Finally, with significant modifications in design, it would have been possible to conduct the study as experimental rather than comparative-descriptive research. The rejection of this approach was based on a belief that the requirements of sound experimental research would have produced findings far more narrow in scope than are presented here. The intent was to produce a wide range of general findings upon which a new theory of police leadership and management could be developed. In this respect, the present research has a certain phenomenological character that has proven to be quite helpful in the researcher's effort to construct the new model.

Instrumentation

The development of the PLPS survey instrument was guided by the researcher's 22 years in law enforcement, his work as an organizational consultant, and a thorough review of the literature of organizational leadership and management of police administration. The PLPS was field tested and subjected to the reviews of two expert panels and to the analysis of respected survey research methodologists. Changes in survey design and in specific items were made in response to criticism offered during this design phase.

Results of the survey were put to several tests, each of which confirmed either the internal consistency (reliability of the instrument) or the validity of the findings.

On the basis of the foregoing, it is concluded that the PLPS offers an important new research tool in the effort to understand, if not to diagnose and improve, police leadership practices in America's big cities. It is also suggested that with minor modifications, the instrument also can be made useful for police agencies serving populations of under 200,000, as well as other organizations.

Relevance and Utility of the PLPS Scales: Conclusions

The use of correlation coefficients on all four scales of the PLPS confirmed reliability of the survey instrument. Although a factor analysis motivated a significant modification of the PLPS, it is concluded that each of the four original scales offers a relevant and useful way to gauge the values and the practices of big-city police chiefs. That conclusion is based on the fact that the "manager" scale, which produced the lowest combined Cronbach alpha of the four, was still quite robust at .897.

The rotated factor analysis did reveal, however, that 35 of the 100 items of the PLPS did not load parsimoniously within their assigned scales. Further, a total of nine factors were found to underlie the survey scales, four from the leadership variables and five from the management variables.

It is concluded from both the reliability and the factor analyses that the elimination—or the modification—of these 35 items was necessary if the PLPS is to realize its full potential as a relevant and useful instrument for assessing police leadership and management practices.

Suggestions for Future Research

As comparative-descriptive research, this study has produced a great deal of information and provided a basis upon which a new model for police executive leadership and executive management could be formulated. But its limitations are also apparent. Out of those limitations come the following recommendations.

First, it is suggested that future research include a field experiment. If it is possible, for example, to find two police departments, one willing to experiment with the model and the other willing to serve as a control, it would be worthwhile to test the effects using a variety of indices of organizational effectiveness, efficiency, and morale, as well as indications of changes in community-police relations.

Second, this research could be repeated. Because it is the first to employ the PLPS, it would be interesting to see whether the same methodology and instrumentation—applied perhaps to police departments serving cities of 100,000 to 199,999 people—would produce similar or different results. Pure replication, using the same population, could be done, but it is unlikely that the departments would be as cooperative the second time around.

Third, if the research were replicated, the population could be expanded to determine the opinions and observations of a broader audience: all assistants, for example, rather than just two; middle managers; first-line supervisors; rank-and-file employees or the employee association's board of directors; city managers; mayors; and community members.

Fourth, the PLPS could be modified to ask the chiefs to describe their behavior, rather than their values and their beliefs.

Fifth, ethnographic research, in which the researcher "tags along" with the chief executive for a significant period, could produce important results. Observing and classifying all tasks and duties performed as belonging either to the leadership or to the management category would provide firsthand information on how police chiefs spend their days.

Finally, future research using the PLPS should consider the use of "stem reversals" for the questions, as well as employing only the 65 questions of the Leader-34 scale and the Manager-31 scale.

Appendix B

INSTRUMENTS USED IN THE POLICE LEADERSHIP PRACTICES SURVEY

The survey used two instruments (questionnaires)—one for police chief executives, the other for those reporting to the chief executives. The two instruments were worded almost identically: chiefs were asked to record their professed values whereas assistants were requested to record observations of their chiefs' actual behavior.

For example, the first item on the chiefs' survey instrument reads, "I believe the police chief executive should encourage questioning and criticism of agency policies." The assistants' version reads, "I perceive that my boss encourages questioning and criticism of agency policies."

Because the two survey instruments parallel one another very closely, only the chiefs' version is reprinted below.

POLICE LEADERSHIP PRACTICES SURVEY
(For the Chief Executive)

This survey is part of an effort to learn more about the leadership practices and the opinions of big-city police chief executives. Please do not put your name on this questionnaire. The identification number in the upper right-hand corner is for purposes of analysis only. Your name will not be associated in any way with the information you provide, and all responses will be held in the strictest confidence. The information you do provide, however, is vital to the research so your cooperation is greatly appreciated. Feel free to use the comments section to clarify any of the information below.

a. Age:_____

b. Sex: M___ F___

c. Race: Asian__ Black__ Hispanic__ Non-Hispanic White__

d. Please circle highest level of education attained:
   8 9 10 11 12 13 14 15 16 17 18+ Degree:_____

e. My agency serves a population of:_____

f. My agency serves a jurisdiction of:_____ square miles

g. Number of sworn personnel:_____

h. Number of nonsworn personnel:_____

i. Total personnel, including reserves or auxiliary police:_____

j. My agency is: centralized_____ decentralized_____

k. My title or rank:_____

l. I was appointed by: Mayor___ Council___ City Manager___

m. I have been in law enforcement for: ___years, ___months

n. I have been chief executive of my agency for: ___years, ___months.

Comments:
_____
_____
_____
_____

Chief Executive Survey

Following is a series of statements concerning leadership and management in a law enforcement agency. You are asked to circle the number that most accurately reflects your personal feelings or opinions about each statement. As with similar surveys, there are no right or wrong answers so please work quickly through each item. Typically, the first impression is the most authentic reflection of how one feels about a given statement.

In responding, you are asked to consider the degree of *personal attention* you would give each function or task. A "5" indicates the strongest possible agreement, a "1" means the strongest possible disagreement.

Please be sure to *circle a number for each statement.* Once again, your opinions will be held strictly confidential. When you have completed the survey, please mail it to me in the enclosed envelope. Thank you very much for your help.

I BELIEVE THE POLICE EXECUTIVE SHOULD:

		STRONGLY AGREE				STRONGLY DISAGREE
1.	Encourage questioning and criticism of agency policies.	5	4	3	2	1
2.	Do everything possible to facilitate the work of the agency's employees.	5	4	3	2	1
3.	Know and understand contemporary management and leadership theory.	5	4	3	2	1
4.	Be intimately involved in the development of the budget.	5	4	3	2	1
5.	Invite citizen input on agency policies.	5	4	3	2	1

		STRONGLY AGREE				STRONGLY DISAGREE
6.	Challenge people in the organization to do better.	5	4	3	2	1
7.	Personally inspect offices periodically.	5	4	3	2	1
8.	Be seen as analytical.	5	4	3	2	1
9.	Personally greet all new employees.	5	4	3	2	1
10.	Work to develop leadership capabilities throughout the supervisory ranks.	5	4	3	2	1
11.	Personally set the organization's priorities for enforcement and service.	5	4	3	2	1
12.	Be seen as the agency's primary problem solver.	5	4	3	2	1
13.	Address each new academy class.	5	4	3	2	1
14.	Make clear his or her personal expectations for effective performance.	5	4	3	2	1
15.	Run agency meetings that he or she attends.	5	4	3	2	1
16.	Maintain organizational control at all times.	5	4	3	2	1
17.	Delegate day-to-day responsibility for management of the agency to a trusted subordinate.	5	4	3	2	1
18.	Develop in his or her subordinates a strong sense of personal responsibility for good work.	5	4	3	2	1

		STRONGLY AGREE			STRONGLY DISAGREE	
19.	Communicate clear expectations for professional conduct of all employees.	5	4	3	2	1
20.	Spend as much time as possible in the office, attending to the business of the agency.	5	4	3	2	1
21.	Meet often with community leaders.	5	4	3	2	1
22.	Be open to community feedback on agency performance.	5	4	3	2	1
23.	Personally inspect uniformed personnel from time to time.	5	4	3	2	1
24.	Be intimately familiar with laws enforced by his or her officers.	5	4	3	2	1
25.	Approach his or her work in an intuitive and creative way.	5	4	3	2	1
26.	Enlist the support of others in setting agency objectives.	5	4	3	2	1
27.	Be intimately involved in the agency's planning process.	5	4	3	2	1
28.	Be able to answer immediately questions from his or her boss(es) about police operations.	5	4	3	2	1
29.	Visit families of officers killed or severely injured on the job.	5	4	3	2	1
30.	Encourage openness and honesty throughout the organization.	5	4	3	2	1
31.	Ensure that all agency personnel are given relevant education and training.	5	4	3	2	1

		STRONGLY AGREE			STRONGLY DISAGREE	
32.	Have constantly up-to-date information about the agency's budget status.	5	4	3	2	1
33.	Build a strong sense of team spirit and teamwork throughout the agency.	5	4	3	2	1
34.	Develop and encourage the use of an "open door" policy.	5	4	3	2	1
35.	Set standards of performance and conduct for all personnel.	5	4	3	2	1
36.	Be known as one who effectively organizes tasks.	5	4	3	2	1
37.	Ride along with patrol officers from time to time.	5	4	3	2	1
38.	Ensure the health, safety, and well-being of the work force.	5	4	3	2	1
39.	Personally monitor and control per capita costs of policing.	5	4	3	2	1
40.	Review all nonroutine expenditures.	5	4	3	2	1
41.	Act as a model of what is expected of all personnel.	5	4	3	2	1
42.	Elicit feedback from the rank and file on agency policies and practices.	5	4	3	2	1
43.	Know at all times what is going on in the agency.	5	4	3	2	1
44.	Have an aide represent him or her at most ceremonial functions.	5	4	3	2	1

		STRONGLY AGREE				STRONGLY DISAGREE
45.	Wear the agency's uniform periodically.	5	4	3	2	1
46.	Ensure that all safety equipment is complete and up to date.	5	4	3	2	1
47.	Define the mission and objectives of the agency.	5	4	3	2	1
48.	Coordinate personally the major activities of the organization.	5	4	3	2	1
49.	Celebrate the accomplishments of employees.	5	4	3	2	1
50.	Use all available means to communicate with employees at all levels.	5	4	3	2	1
51.	Establish and maintain a reasonable span of control for all supervisors.	5	4	3	2	1
52.	Be seen as a neutral and objective manager.	5	4	3	2	1
53.	Recognize publicly the excellent and/or heroic work of employees.	5	4	3	2	1
54.	Be known as one who practices what he or she preaches.	5	4	3	2	1
55.	Ensure that the vehicle fleet is complete, clean, and efficiently maintained.	5	4	3	2	1
56.	Set precise work output standards for employees.	5	4	3	2	1

		STRONGLY AGREE			STRONGLY DISAGREE	
57.	Share with others in the organization his or her true feelings about agency issues.	5	4	3	2	1
58.	Make clear his or her personal expectations for nondiscriminatory behavior.	5	4	3	2	1
59.	Monitor the police radio periodically.	5	4	3	2	1
60.	Sign off on all correspondence leaving the agency.	5	4	3	2	1
61.	Attend many community meetings on crime and police practices.	5	4	3	2	1
62.	Correct or dismiss poor performers.	5	4	3	2	1
63.	Set specific objectives for units.	5	4	3	2	1
64.	Be thoroughly familiar with the agency's computer programs.	5	4	3	2	1
65.	Send cards to injured or ill employees.	5	4	3	2	1
66.	Create a hospitable work environment.	5	4	3	2	1
67.	Set and monitor standards for detective case cancellations.	5	4	3	2	1
68.	Have more technical expertise than his or her subordinates.	5	4	3	2	1
69.	Place a high value on diversity of opinion within the organization.	5	4	3	2	1

		STRONGLY AGREE				STRONGLY DISAGREE
70.	Be seen as an enthusiastic promoter of the organization.	5	4	3	2	1
71.	Evaluate systematically the overall performance of the organization.	5	4	3	2	1
72.	Approach his or her work in a logical, orderly, and unemotional fashion.	5	4	3	2	1
73.	Visit hospitalized members.	5	4	3	2	1
74.	Be seen by his or her employees as absolutely honest.	5	4	3	2	1
75.	Personally direct the activities of his or her immediate subordinates.	5	4	3	2	1
76.	Personally control the key managerial processes of the agency.	5	4	3	2	1
77.	Make frequent visits to units throughout the organization.	5	4	3	2	1
78.	Attend supervisors meetings from time to time.	5	4	3	2	1
79.	Set and enforce an expectation that all employees follow the chain of command.	5	4	3	2	1
80.	Be seen as a good "detail" person.	5	4	3	2	1
81.	Inspire throughout the organization a shared vision of the future.	5	4	3	2	1
82.	Go to the scene of all officer-involved shootings that result in death.	5	4	3	2	1

		STRONGLY AGREE				STRONGLY DISAGREE
83.	Be seen as a strong advocate of management's prerogatives in relations with the employees association or union.	5	4	3	2	1
84.	Be able to answer immediately most work-related technical questions.	5	4	3	2	1
85.	Encourage risk taking by employees at all levels.	5	4	3	2	1
86.	Encourage initiative throughout the organization.	5	4	3	2	1
87.	Participate personally in the work of developing agency policies.	5	4	3	2	1
88.	Be responsible for dispensing the agency's narcotics "buy money."	5	4	3	2	1
89.	Personally meet with employees who are retiring.	5	4	3	2	1
90.	Encourage new ideas by all members of the agency.	5	4	3	2	1
91.	Be responsible for work flow throughout the agency.	5	4	3	2	1
92.	Cultivate an attitude that he or she is the person most responsible for how things are going in the agency.	5	4	3	2	1
93.	Share responsibility for organizational leadership.	5	4	3	2	1

		STRONGLY AGREE				STRONGLY DISAGREE
94.	Meet often with chief executives of other law enforcement agencies in the area.	5	4	3	2	1
95.	Be responsible for deciding how and where resources will be allocated.	5	4	3	2	1
96.	Set clear and unequivocal lines of authority throughout the agency.	5	4	3	2	1
97.	Master both organizational and community political skills.	5	4	3	2	1
98.	Ride along from time to time on a homicide call-out and/or accompany vice, narcotics, or other detectives in their work.	5	4	3	2	1
99.	Participate in research projects designed to make the agency more efficient.	5	4	3	2	1
100.	Set limits for and personally control overtime expenditures.	5	4	3	2	1
			*	*	*	

If you would like a summary of the results of this research, please complete the Survey Results Request form and return it with your completed questionnaire. (These forms will be separated from the individual surveys before the results are tabulated.)

Thank you again for your help.

Police Executive Research Forum

The Police Executive Research Forum (PERF) is a national professional association of chief executives of large city, county and state police departments. PERF's purpose is to improve the delivery of police services and the effectiveness of crime control through several means:

- the exercise of strong national leadership;
- public debate of police and criminal justice issues;
- research and policy development; and
- the provision of vital management leadership services to police agencies.

PERF members are selected on the basis of their commitment to PERF's purpose and principles. The principles that guide the Police Executive Research Forum are:

- Research, experimentation and exchange of ideas through public discussion and debate are paths for development of a professional body of knowledge about policing;
- Substantial and purposeful academic study is a prerequisite for acquiring, understanding and adding to the body of knowledge of professional police management;
- Maintenance of the highest standards of ethics and integrity is imperative in the improvement of policing;
- The police must, within the limits of the law, be responsible and accountable to citizens as the ultimate source of police authority; and
- The principles embodied in the Constitution are the foundation of policing.